THIS BEAUTIFUL ESCAPE

VOLUME ONE

This Beautiful Escape
Volume One
Copyright © 2015 1st Edition

Table of Contents

Contributors' Favorite Quotes

"I am STRONG because I know my Weakness. I am BEAUTIFUL because I am aware of my Flaws. I am FEARLESS because I learn to recognise illusion from Real. I am WISE because I learn from my Mistakes. I am a LOVER because I have felt Hate and I can LAUGH because I have known Sadness."

- Unknown

"No matter how bad a state of mind you may get into, if you keep strong and hold out, eventually the floating clouds must vanish and the withering wind must cease."

- Dogen Zenjii (JD Hawkins)

"I have not failed. I've just found 10,000 ways that won't work."

- Thomas A. Edison - (Bella Jeanisse)

"The best and most beautiful things in the world cannot be seen or even touched -- they must be felt with the heart."

- Helen Keller (Jenna Galicki)

"If you don't like the truth, then don't make it the truth."

- JW Snootz

Foreword by Melissa Ann

The day we are born we are given the greatest gift in the world …
Life. Our gift at first is pristine and perfectly wrapped with sparkles
and a perfectly tied bow, but over time the paper starts to tear, the
sparkles fade and the bow becomes threadbare. Instead of watching
this gift fade away you need to take it and make it new again. Tape
up all those little tears, add your own sparkles and tie a brand new
bow. It might not be as perfect as it was the day you were born but
you try to make the most with what you have. We are only given one
life. We can't go to Walmart and buy a new one. Choose to take this
life and embrace it. –Melissa Ann–

In 2005 I was diagnosed with Episodic Ataxia. I can't really say that
the diagnosis was life-altering because I've lived with it since birth. I
am limited in ways the average person may not be, but learning to
adapt and adjust has become a fine art that I have mastered. I may
not be able to play sports or ride rollercoasters, but I have been given
the gift of writing. A good friend told me that I write from my soul. I
want people to feel. I believe it is my purpose to use this gift to help
others and it is for this reason "This Beautiful Escape" was created.

I am truly humbled by the response this project has received. To
experience all these authors from different genres coming together,
sharing a piece of their soul to give others hope, warms my heart. I
truly hope that you, the reader, are as touched reading these words as
I am. We are not only inspiring people but we are also raising
awareness of an illness that is often misdiagnosed. All proceeds will
be donated directly to Ataxia Canada and used for research in
finding a cure. Thank you for your support.

LIVING WITH ATAXIA

by

Melissa Ann

"Life isn't about waiting for the storm to pass … it's learning to dance in the rain."

- Vivian Greene

I dedicate my story to my children. Their inner-light shines brightly with their empathetic spirit.

My body feels as though it is encased in cement. Every movement is slow, unpredictable and saps me of energy. If I could just sleep my episode would subside but I have no choice, life beckons me. I mentally prepare myself for the journey to the kitchen which is at the opposite end of the house from my bedroom. I don't live in a mansion but even the shortest distance requires stamina, and a strategic plan to get there. I sit at the edge of my bed and look for the nearest object I can hang on to. It's like a video game; instead of using platforms to jump on to reach the other side of the room, it's various objects in the house like chairs, walls or tables that you can use to prevent you from falling and harming yourself. I shuffle along the hallway, willing my feet to move as they should but to no avail. I want my feet to move one way but my brain commands them to move another. The harder I concentrate the more erratic my movements become. Have you ever tried to walk from one side of the pool to another? Your body feels heavy, your movements are slow and by the time you reach the other side you are fatigued. This is how I can best describe my journey to the kitchen.

I attempt to sneak by my children's rooms because I don't want them to see me like this. If I am at a party or an event and I have an episode I will sit and not engage people with the hope it will pass. I don't want people's sympathy and for those that don't know me… I don't want them to think I am intoxicated. To an outsider that's what it looks like; my speech is slurred, my movements erratic and my balance unpredictable. Although my children know about my illness, I don't want them to see me weak and helpless. I am their mother, it is I that needs to take care of them, not the other way around.

My journey to the kitchen was one battle I won but cooking is a whole new ball of wax. Something that should only take me a half hour to prepare and make will oftentimes take me twice as long, even three times the amount of time. I lean against the counter as I fry the hamburger, I stir the meat in the frying pan to prevent burning… but it's at that moment my hand decides to spasm and some of the contents in the pan spill on the stove. I turn off the element and pray that it won't start smoking or worse catch fire. I whip the spoon I had used across the room and sink into the nearest chair and weep. Tears are streaming down my face and sobs are wracking my body and I can't stop. I am so exhausted. I don't want to fight my body any more. I can't even cook a simple meal to feed my children. I feel arms surround me and it's my daughter. I can see the fear and concern in her eyes, which only makes me cry more. My children deserve a mother that can go out and play with them, go on school trips with them not one that has a body that doesn't always work.

I have to remind myself that things could always be worse. I need to not focus on what I can't do but focus on what I can. I might not always have the use of my body but I have my mind. I can write stories to entertain, to send a message. I have my heart; to love and spread love.

Individuals who've known pain, loss and struggle always appreciate what they have more and have sympathetic hearts.

Without struggle we wouldn't learn to appreciate life.

The best thing about having this illness is that my children have empathetic hearts. Children are the future and maybe through their life experiences they can use this wonderful virtue to help change the world.

Always remember we all have a purpose. There will be days you break down and cry and forget what that reason is and that's okay. What's important is that you get up again. Start that climb up the mountain and when you reach the top look at the world around you. You will realize in the grand scheme of things that your problems are small. We only have one life; embrace it, live it, love it.

ATAXIA

by

Monica May

"Our greatest weakness lies in giving up. The most certain way to succeed is always to try just one more time."

- Thomas A. Edison

I dedicate this to my grandmother, grandfather, and two uncles. You never gave up and you fought till the end showing us all how to live.

How did it feel to grow up in an Ataxia family? What did it feel like to always have someone dying in your family? Yep, I have had people actually ask me those questions. And this is what I have to say to that.

It felt amazing to grow up in an Ataxia family. To tell you the truth, as a kid, I had no clue anyone was dying around me. I knew my uncle walked funny, but man, he was one of the best uncles ever. He would sneak us out for a walk to the corner candy store, and we would hide the candy under his bed so my grandmother would not find it. He loved us so much. He pretended we were his children, and in the end, he would tell the nurses he had three children and a wife with the same name as my mother. She would just giggle and go along with it because it made him happy to dream he had a family.

My grandmother was the strongest person I knew—the ultimate caregiver—and I will always continue to strive to be like her. She had more faith than one would know what to do with, and she had been dealt a difficult hand. She had a husband and two of her six children with a terminal illness. So who am I to doubt God's decision? Ataxia taught me not to whine about nonsense. My grandmother taught her children to help out when they could and live their lives to the fullest because you never knew when it would be taken away. Now that was not an exact quote from her, but it was the message I received by her example because Ataxia really was not discussed in our family. We all knew it was there, but we were not allowed to let it dictate our lives.

No one in our family had ever been tested for it that I know of. At one point, my grandmother had asked her youngest son to get tested before he married and had children. She had suspicions that he may have the ill-fated disease. I chuckled when I thought of that particular uncle. He was always the cool uncle—the really handsome one with the motorcycle in the early 80s. Yeah, that was him. My sister and I loved to play the flip-flop game with him. His rule was if we could pull his flip-flop off his foot, we could have the entire can of his big red and white striped peppermints. I just remember him as strong because we never could get that damn flip-flop off and we would pull together. But he still gave us one candy for trying, but he never gave us the entire can. He would say you have to earn it, and I'm not just going to give it to you because you want it. Well, he had lied to my grandmother and said he had been tested to ease her mind. He and his fiancée had decided they didn't want to know. They loved each other, and they did not want a disease that may or may not show up until his forties or fifties get in the way. They married and had two sons. I'm sure he does not regret his two boys that are now men with children of their own. He is now in his mid-fifties and has been living with Ataxia for about twenty years. Today I could get his flip-flop off with ease, due to Ataxia. And if I told you it was not a concern while I was pregnant with my own children, I would be lying to you. But after some rationalization, I realized God will give me what he gives me and I will accept it. That is what the disease and my family has taught me.

My grandmother and aunts would do things that just did not make sense to me as a kid. Not until I had my own children and became a mature woman did I realize why they would do the things they did. They would eat gross food like canned cranberry because it was my uncle's favorite and he could no longer eat it. One aunt ran in marathons because two of her brothers could not. They would suck up little bumps and bruises or aches and pains and give it up to their father that had since passed while they wished he were here to complain about a tired back from doing yard work. And now the same type of words come right out of my mouth without thought. My daughter had hurt her foot in a very minor way, and she cried, complained, and over-exaggerated to no end. My response was to say, "Your great-grandfather and two uncles only wish they could complain about a sore ankle from being able to run around and play basketball for two hours." Yeah, it gets them thinking about how thankful they should be.

What Ataxia taught us through the years made our family indestructible when the parish we lived in was destroyed by Hurricane Katrina in 2005. We all lost our homes and everything in them. My grandmother, three of her children, all seven of her grandchildren, and four of her great-grandchildren all lost their homes. So what if we lost our house and everything in it. It was tough at first, but we stood up and realized we had insurance and needed to move on. We were thankful no one in our family stayed and tried to ride the storm out and everyone was okay. My mother took in my aging grandmother, her mother-in-law, and my uncle, her brother-in-law who had Ataxia, and my mother took care of them. While my father shows no signs of having Ataxia, my mother always mimicked her mother-in-law in caretaking and took care of her with a kind heart and dignity until the end.

So the moral of the story is that growing up with Ataxia around me has made me a strong woman, a caring mother, and most of all, it made me a fighter for all I believe and all I think is right.

NEW BEGINNINGS

by

David S. Scott

"It matters not how strait the gate,

How charged with punishment the scroll.

I am the master of my fate.

I am the captain of my soul."

- William Ernest Henley

To Steph, the love of my life. Each day brings our new beginning.

The room must have been lit, but all I remember is darkness. I gazed down at my wife's tearstained face. I was angry, angry at losing control. Furious at not being able to protect her, to save her from this pain. My chest ached just to look at her.

The steady beep of the monitors broke into my awareness. The sound pierced my brain. My fists clenched. I tried to hold the rage I felt inside, to not let her see … but it was no use. She could see it in the tightness of my jaw, in the stiffness of my hands. I forced myself to relax.

I rolled my chair closer to her, placed my hand over hers. I forced my mouth into a smile that didn't reach my eyes.

"Valerie, I'm sorry. I'd do anything to change things. We can try again."

Tears filled her beautiful blue eyes. Shit. I'd said the wrong thing. I was fucking good at that. I slid off the chair, falling on my knees before her. "I'm sorry, Val. I'm so sorry." I couldn't take looking at her any longer. I dropped my forehead onto the side of her hospital bed. She pulled her hand away, running her fingers through my hair.

God damn it. She's the one who just had surgery, the one who had to find out she was pregnant and that it was ectopic all in the same day … yet she is the one comforting me. This won't do. I jerked my face back up to look at her again and grabbed her fingers in mine.

"It's okay, Daniel. I know you didn't mean that like it came out. It's just … it's too soon."

I kissed her fingers, squeezed her hand. "I know. I almost lost you today. I've never been more terrified. Valerie, I–I can't lose you."

"You didn't almost lose me. I'm–I'll be okay."

"I was standing right there. I heard the doctor say it was good they found out the bab–that it was stuck in your tubes this early. I heard him say if they hadn't you could have fucking died. Don't try to make light of this now."

I could see the defeat in her eyes and I hated myself for it. I skimmed my thumb over her knuckles and wracked my brain to think of some magical way to fix everything. There was nothing. Nothing I could do. I hated feeling helpless.

The nurses came in to give her the discharge paperwork and I left to go bring the car around. The hallways seemed dark and foreboding to my tormented mind. I'm sure people must have greeted me and that the lights were glowing brightly, but to me the world felt straight out of a horror movie.

The drive home was silent and awkward, punctuated by Valarie's quiet sobbing. I held her hand and tried to soothe her as best I could.

Days turned into weeks, which turned into months. Many nights I heard my beloved Valerie crying in the middle of the night when she thought I was asleep. My heart was broken beyond repair for her. I couldn't fight this enemy. I couldn't save her.

Things were strained between us. Sometimes something like a spark was there, sometimes we were like strangers. Gone was the carefree lovemaking we once shared. Left in its place was fear and pain. Something had to give.

Six months after my wife's surgery, we received a strange phone call from a young woman. Her name was Clarissa; she sounded upset and asked to meet with us privately.

She arrived later that day, shaking and distressed. We invited her into our home, and Valerie quickly prepared her a glass of tea.

"I … I'm sure you're wondering why I asked to meet with you."

"Indeed," I said, pretending not to notice Valerie glaring daggers at me for my perceived rudeness.

"Um, yes, well … do you remember Reverend Carlson?"

I looked to Valerie, but she looked as confused as I felt. I shook my head. "I'm sorry, young lady, you seem to have us at a loss."

"He was old and wrinkled, but had kind blue eyes that soothed me when I looked into them. He said he knew you; that he had prayed with you at the hospital. He gave me your names; I looked you up in the phone book."

A jolt of shock and dread shot down my spine as the events of that day flooded my system. I couldn't bring myself to look at my wife's face. Instead, I stared at Clarissa, my mind struggling to understand what she was saying.

"It … it's been a long time," said Valerie. "I don't think I ever even knew his name."

"What's this about?" I demanded.

She gripped her cup of tea and stared at the floor. "I'm pregnant. I went to the hospital last week because of severe illness, and found out that was why. I … I …"

Valerie's face was a mask of stone. "Congratulations."

"Thanks," she said absently as she plucked at imaginary lint on her pants. "But listen … it's not like that. I wasn't bragging, I'm … I was …" she trailed off, her eyes welling with tears and her cheeks darkening in shame.

I stared helplessly at her, at a loss for words. She continued to scratch at her clothing, as tears streamed down her face.

"I didn't mean to … I thought he wouldn't … wouldn't. He seemed like a nice guy, I never expected to be …"

"Raped," Valerie whispered. At Clarissa's shuddering nod, Valerie moved to her side and wrapped her arms around her. "I'm so sorry."

Clarissa pulled away, wiping her tears and taking a deep breath. "When I was at the hospital, I begged for them to end it, even as I loathed myself for it. I can't afford to raise a child, I have no family to speak of … and I can't be reminded daily of what happened. I was lost, confused. I didn't want to … to have an a–"

She swiped at her face with shaky hands, tears quickly replacing the ones she removed before continuing. "… but I didn't see any other option. I knew I would hate myself forever, but what choice did I have? Reverend Carlson came to me. We talked, he listened to me and we prayed together. Before he left, he gave me your names and told me that I should find you, that he had a feeling we were the answer to each other's prayers."

"What? How? What did he tell you about us?" I asked.

"Not much, only that you were hurting and he felt our paths were connected."

Valerie paled. "I'm afraid I still don't understand."

"Do you have any children?"

No," I answered, my voice hoarse.

"Would you like one?"

***

"What do you think?"

We had just gotten our strange houseguest out the door with the promise we would call her with our decision as soon as possible. Valerie turned to me, looking as lost and confused as I felt.

"I think she's trying to put on a brave face, but she is terrified." Valerie picked at the ends of her long, curly hair. "I feel for her."

"I agree, but that wasn't my question. Should we do it?"

She stared helplessly at me. "How can we make a life-changing decision in a matter of moments?"

I shrugged. "Not any different from deciding to try to have a child ourselves. What does your gut say?"

She bit her lip. "I want to help her, but I just don't know." We sat in silence, digesting our decision. At length, Valerie sighed. "It all seems so farfetched, but I believe her. She needs help. This child wouldn't be ours though, Daniel. It's not the same and it wouldn't replace what we lost."

"Of course not. But just because this child isn't ours, does it deserve any less of a chance at a good life with a loving family?"

Valerie looked up then, her eyes boring into mine. "You think we should do it."

I scratched the back of my head. "I think … I think I couldn't live with myself if we said no and she did something she'd regret the rest of her life. I think we could love this child as our own. I think it would tempt karma to say no. It's been six months, and this stranger to us remembered our names. It's … it's fate."

Valerie threw her arms around my neck. "I love you madly, you know? Only you would look at this bizarre situation and call it fate." She raised up on her tiptoes, pulling my head down toward hers.

"I love you, too." I captured her lips in mine. My tongue tangled with hers, my fingers fumbled at her clothes. It had been far too long since we had been hot for each other like this. She moaned into my mouth, the sound sending blood rushing into my cock, which strained against my pants and begged for release.

"Oh, Valerie, I–"

I cut off my own sentence to bite and suck on her lower lip. Our breaths came in shuddering gasps. I was about to lead her into our bedroom when she dropped to her knees before me and struggled with the zipper to my pants. She ran her nails over my contained erection, sending lightning ricocheting throughout my body. I groaned and unsnapped the button, not even daring to breathe as she pulled the zipper down and freed my throbbing cock. She palmed it, skimming her hand teasingly over my length as she gently stroked me. My dick jerked into her hand as she touched me and she grinned deviously up at me.

"Uh oh," she breathed. "Looks like this needs some attention. Poor thing, looks like it hurts from being so swollen."

I could only nod in response. She was killing me with all the teasing.

She leaned forward and slowly, gently licked the tip. My breath hissed out in a ragged gasp. It had been too long since we were like this, and I was desperate for her. Her hand gripped me more firmly, squeezing, milking me as her lips closed around my throbbing head.

"Fuck, Valerie. Oh my God, like that." My eyes tried to roll back in my head but I forced them to stay on her, my beautiful wife with the caramel colored curls. I moaned deep in my throat. "Suck me."

She licked her tongue along the sensitive vein on the underside of my cock, then hollowed her cheeks and took me deep into her hot mouth, sucking hard. My hips jutted forward of their own volition. I gripped her hair in my fingers, tightening them reflexively and pulling lightly as I held her right where I wanted her. She slid her mouth up and down the shaft, her hand working me at the base where her mouth couldn't reach.

Her other hand came up and cupped my balls, massaging me, squeezing gently. I was getting close to orgasm … but I couldn't yet. I didn't want to come in her mouth. I just needed to bring myself to stop her. She pumped me harder, deeper. The tip of my cock bumped the back of her throat and I let out a strangled gasp, yanking on her hair.

She released me, breathing hard. "Why'd you stop me?"

I struggled to find my voice. "Because it was too fucking good. I would have come in your mouth."

"Good." She reached for me but I backed away.

"No." I helped her to her feet and gave her a short, bruising kiss. Her lips were so soft, so swollen after she had been sucking me. "Not this time. I want to come inside you, with you screaming my name."

I considered taking her to our bedroom but decided we wouldn't make it. I pushed her into the nearby wall, cushioning her head with my hand.

"Do you know what you do to me?" I growled, shoving her jeans and panties down. She kicked them off and then I was on her again, my hand reaching under her shirt to fondle her breasts.

She slid her hand around my cock and squeezed as she stood on her tiptoes to kiss me. "I think I have a pretty good idea."

"Oh, baby, you have *no* idea. I've missed this. Come here." I reached down to grab her by the ass and lifted her up. She locked her legs around my waist, then I lined myself up and plunged deep inside her.

"Oh, fuck! Yes, Daniel, oh God."

I used the wall to help brace her, then drove myself into her again and again. She wrapped her arms around me and bit my neck, sucking my flesh into her mouth to muffle her screams. The sharp pain only served to drive me even more wild for her. She met my thrusts by grinding herself on me, her nails clawed at my back and neck. I shifted her hips forward, allowing me to penetrate her even deeper.

"Daniel, don't stop. Don't ever stop, oh fuck … just like that. Oh God, I'm so close."

I pressed her harder into the wall and reached my hand between us to rub her clit. She threw her head back, bumping hard into the wall as she cried out.

"Yes, come for me, Valerie," I panted. "Do it. I want to hear you fucking scream for me."

"Oh God, oh God, Daniel, yes. I'm coming. Fuck! Daniel!" Her legs quivered around me as I felt her pussy begin to pulse around my cock, squeezing me deliciously, encouragingly. I buried myself into her as far as I could, waves of bliss rhythmically sweeping over my body. Goosebumps raced along my arms and I trembled as we held each other tight, crushingly, as we rode out our orgasms together.

Finally, I set her down and kissed her on the forehead. "I love you, Val."

She smiled up at me. "I love you more."

I stroked my fingers down the side of her face, tucking her hair behind her ear. "Let's do it. We'll have almost the whole pregnancy to prepare."

A huge grin split her face. She found her discarded clothing and pulled them back on, then walked over to the phone. "Clarissa? Yes, hi, this is Valerie Nelson. I was just calling to let you know we, uh, made our decision..."

I watched my wife talk on the phone, feeling happy and contented for the first time in six months. This baby wouldn't be our flesh and blood, but it would be ours, nonetheless. He or she wasn't even born yet and already they were bringing healing to our broken hearts.

***

"What do you mean there isn't anyone with that name who has ever worked here?" I frowned, confused.

I mean that I have been servicing this hospital for the last twenty years. Other clergymen come through here often, but only to tend their own flocks. I, and two other associates, are the only ones who visit residents not belonging to a specific faith here, and only when we are asked for. Generally that happens when someone wants their last rites administered, but sometimes to pray before major surgeries. If you didn't ask for one of us, then we wouldn't have gone. As for this 'Reverend Carlson,' I've never heard of him. In addition, we would never give any patient's name to anyone."

"Clarissa saw him, too. She described him. He was here, I know it," Valerie insisted. "I … we wanted to thank him."

The middle aged preacher's eyes softened. "You were pregnant, weren't you?"

My wife's hands flew to her belly protectively. "I lost that one, yes. He prayed with us."

"I have no way of getting in touch with him for you. I'm sorry."

"I thought you said there was no one here by that name?" I demanded.

"There isn't."

"I thought a preacher was here to help people. You just speak in riddles."

He walked to the door to his office and shut it, closing us off from the rest of the hospital. A shiver ran down my spine.

"I've heard stories several times throughout the years of an elderly man who helps to soothe grieving mothers. There are several legends. I've never seen him and, frankly, I've always dismissed such things as the mind's way to help heal. There is no one here named Reverend Carlson. There has not been anyone here by that name in the last twenty years at least."

"Are you trying to tell us he is a ghost?" I scoffed.

"I don't believe in ghosts, Mr. Nelson. I believe that once we die, our spirits are judged and spend eternity in either heaven or hell.

Hospitals are famous for ghost stories, but I don't believe a single one."

Valerie wiped tears from her eyes. "Not a ghost. He was our guardian angel. Good day, Reverend."

Things had progressed quickly over the last few months. We had met with a lawyer to draw up adoption paperwork, and we had begun to prepare the nursery for not only one baby, but two. Only a couple of weeks after we'd agreed to adopt Clarissa's baby, Valerie tested positive yet again.

After that had come a blur of tests, ultrasounds, and bloodwork. We were both terrified of a repeat ectopic, but every test came back normal. About a month after that fateful day we had agreed to adopt, we were able to see our baby's heartbeat for the first time.

Clarissa had been afraid we were going to change our minds, but we assured her that we had agreed and we wouldn't fail her. Her child and ours would be raised as siblings, and would be as close as twins.

That horrible day in the hospital threatened to be our ruin, but love and hope eventually prevailed. We'll never forget the child whom was taken from us, or the heartache and horror that accompanied it, but we know that we have to let go, to heal, and to move forward … always forward.

I do not know whom Reverend Carlson was. Maybe he was a ghost, maybe an angel. Perhaps he was just a random flesh and blood preacher who happened to be in the right place at the right time. It doesn't matter. If I ever see him again, I will shake his hand and tell him thank you.

As we look toward our future, I realize that dwelling in the past is no way to heal. Our experiences wound us, shape us, and make us who we are … but they don't have to define us. We have to let it go, live in the moment and look to the future. Every day is a chance at a new beginning.

EMOTIONS OF LOVE

by

Ethan Radcliff

"Love me or hate me

both are in my favor...

If you love me,

I'll always be in your heart...

If you hate me,

I'll always be in your mind."

- Shakespeare

Emotions of Love

Treasured emotions grow
My heart is in tow
I've been hurt and deserted
Knowing what it's like to be hurting
Yet I've learned to love again
And you may too my friend

Waking each day to the sun
Trying to make the day fun
Learning to treat others as one
Giving not taking under the gun
Loving others leaning not to shun
Those less fortunate ones

We must learn to see the beauty
In all things real and free
We nurture our feelings to be
Deep and overpowering
When the clouds cover the sky
Smiles are in order we must try

To see beyond the darkness
And help others see the justice
One man can create with a smile
No tests given not even a trial
Just his love just his life
To the woman he'd take for a wife.

REDEMPTION HEART

by

Muffy Wilson

"What lies behind you and what lies in front of you, pales in comparison to what lies inside of you."

- Ralph Waldo Emerson

We are not the sum of our parts because our parts never stop changing and evolving for the better. Each day, a new message of hope breaks with the dawn. And while we cannot change the past, we can change how we live the present—for it is a gift: a new start, a new chance, and ever-changing opportunity to rewrite our happiness.

This is the story of a young girl—intelligent, inquisitive, engaging—in the fall of her eighteenth year. Blinded by the brilliance of her excitement, her eagerness pressed against the glass of her life, she stood on the precipice before womanhood. She was anxious to plunge, to hold her breath against the trials and tribulations that surely faced her. Whatever lay before her would be hers and hers alone to claim, no longer an extension of someone else's life, and she would survive; she would surely thrive.

She was not a child of privilege, yet she was wealthy from the experience of travel at a very young age. She was not a beauty and yet there was a radiance that glowed from within that attracted people to her. She was not overly intelligent, but curious with an insatiable desire for more of anything and everything she could learn. And she read. She read everything to feed her curiosity and it buoyed her worldliness. What she had was an innate confidence instilled in her by loving parents and protective, indulgent older brothers. She felt—no, she was certain she could do anything she put her mind to work on and prevail. After all, everything lay before her as the wealth that would unfold as her life like glimmering, shimmering jewels was hers for the taking. It was all going to be just that easy.

It is not a story of right or wrong, good or bad. Judgment is not for the living to wage. It is not a story of guilt or innocence, although innocence figures greatly. Nor is it a tale of the road not taken against the one taken instead. It is a story about life and the decisions that shape us. It is a story of redemption. Perhaps by telling this story, it will finally set me free.

I was that young girl struggling to shed the skin of her youthful innocence, anxious to welcome the bounty that would be my life rushing to fill the unspeakable void of experience.

It was the fall of my freshman year at University of California. My older brother and I were attending the Davis campus in northern California and I was living in the dorms while he drove back and forth from home each day. For a year, he was my unspoken safety net. Just knowing he was somewhere on campus gave me that bridge of 'home' security. It was not long before I would be there alone when he was called to go to Viet Nam and fly chopper missions into enemy territory. It was not a new concept to us because my father served proudly in the United States Air Force and was serving there at the time also. Life in the military was the definition of preparing to fight the enemy or fighting the enemy. It was our life.

For a smart girl, I had to take bonehead English which knocked me down a few pegs. I looked around to those who surrounded me in class. I was taking Physics, too, so I was surely smart and I was certain there had been a mistake in my testing transcripts. But, there I was stuck, feeling stupid and helpless to change my class. So, I made up for it in those very first few days in the first week of the semester known as Orientation Week. Every college has "O" week and Davis was no exception.

It was the time when all the freshmen had to go to a slew of scheduled mixers and seminars to learn about the compound, classes, professors, cafeteria, bookstore, athletics and campus transportation. "Meet and Mingle" mixers were scheduled every night and it was exciting. I was pretty full of myself, confident that not only was I smart, in spite of my bonehead English class, having graduated in the top three percent of my class, but I felt beautiful, available, and coming into my own—a woman with no one to answer to but myself. I went to every mixer. I brought a new boy back to my dorm every night—to talk and have coffee and be grown up—nothing more intentionally and deliberately.

I could take my pick of the young men and I found it exciting—intoxicating. But, I'd known that for many years in a juvenile, precocious way. Several of my Dad's pilot buddies had been very solicitous of me and flirtatious, bolstering my self-opinion. I was still trying very hard to be a good girl but I yearned for so much more. So, feeling full of myself and seeking positive reinforcement from the setback of a mandatory English class, I plunged headlong into my freshman year trying to collect as many admirers as possible—to what end and purpose, I did not know. How could I? I was just a girl. I just knew that for once, I wanted to be the popular girl. I wanted to belong and be a part of something that was mine.

I was invited to every party, every dance, every outing by one or another of my 'boys'. I didn't stop to think about it then, but I believe I was trying to make up for how I felt in high school. Growing up in the military, we moved every few years and at every school I attended, I was always 'the new girl'. It only ever mattered in my last two years of high school. I was the newcomer that didn't fit in: smart, pretty, different.

In college, every freshman was a newcomer, not just me, and we all had years ahead of us. I was no longer different. So, I went to every party. I didn't drink much; I never had because it wasn't about drinking and losing control. It was all about belonging and feeling good. In January, I went to a party and met the most handsome man I think I had ever laid eyes on. Jet black hair and the ocean in his eyes, his mouth curled into a confident smile when we met. He was attentive, charming, dazzling, and I fell madly in love, out of the blue as though I had be struck. He was there for the long weekend with buddies visiting friends. His name was Swede. Throughout the weekend, we spent all of our time together. Of course, I knew what was going to happen. I wanted it to happen; I willed it to happen. I had been growing into this moment my entire life.

And I couldn't help myself; I didn't want to help myself. I was so nervous and sick and anxious all rolled up into one. He was tender and kind, gentle and coaxing. He touched and whispered breathing into the tender hot spot of my neck. I melted to his will simply, softly embracing his hard body. It was so special, in the dimly lit room of his friends off campus house. A fish tank gave off a special glow that I could feel inside. It was so unnerving. I never thought he would fit inside me because I was so knotted up, so tight, coiled with desire and anticipation. We spent the whole night together. It was the first time I had ever done that with anyone—and I knew he was the one for me. He went back to SoCal on Monday and we talked as much as possible.

We planned for him to come up a few weeks later and go to Lake Tahoe, skiing. It was going to be glorious, just like in the movies. I was in love and he said he loved me, too. I wrote poems about him and daydreamed about endless days together on the pure white-capped slopes of Lake Tahoe skiing and even more endless nights in his arms by a rolling fire. I was so excited and eager to see him. Then he called and had to cancel. I don't remember why. I don't remember much of the call for the next few minutes. I was crushed. I thought—now it starts, the rejection that I felt as a child, as a 'newcomer' was just inevitable. I felt awful, and all of this happened in a young girl's mind in a split second. Then beyond hope, the dark cloud of despair lifted; he asked me to come to Los Angeles.

I jumped thoughtlessly, carelessly, at the suggestion before he could take it back. I ached to see him, for his touch to reinforce our love. I had to think about it, plan my departure and explanation to anyone who might ask, make arrangements and call him back. How could I refuse? Now, I was really scared…but I was going. I had to go. I had to see him.

Leaving on a Jet Plane by John Denver was a popular song back then. It seemed as though that is all I heard playing on the radio on the long drive all the way down to SF International. I left Davis in the wee hours of the morning for a dawn flight. I was too excited to sleep anyway. He picked me up at the airport and had three friends with him. They had beer and wine coolers in the van. I was nervous, and so happy to see him. I was off put by having so many others with us—so I had a cooler, then another. Soon, we were having so much fun, laughing, driving around, showing me the sights. I remember seeing the La Brea Tar Pits and laughing when they told me there were all sorts of things at the bottom of those black endless pools. It was exhilarating. But, I was getting tired and it was late in the afternoon. I needed to rest before we went out to dinner. I thought we would celebrate our new relationship. We only had the weekend together. And I really wasn't scared anymore. His friends had been nice. Maybe, he was a little scared and needed his friends for moral support. I was charmed by the thought of that…

Pretty soon, the excitement, the long hours without sleep and the trip added up and I was drunk. Not for the first time in my life, but surely more than I had ever been before. Had I really had that much to drink? Dear God, I really couldn't move and I was so tired. I said I needed to lay down for a while before dinner. They took me into one of the downstairs bedrooms and helped me lay down. I couldn't feel anything. Before I knew it, I was in a deep sleep; I thought I could feel my limbs relaxing—the exhaustion and tension just floating away. Then I remember someone in the doorway. It was very dark out and the hall light was bright behind the black figure standing there. I couldn't tell if it was Swede or not, so I asked that he come to me—I didn't feel well. Someone—Swede, I thought— came to me, comforted me, touched me all over. I felt explosive with need. Then I floated away again, but I could not move. I was paralyzed to move or react in any way physically.

The visits, the touching, the tension and my difficulty breathing happened at least four or five times. It wasn't until the next day that I surmised what had happened. I was sore and ached all over; I felt drugged. I had been raped by whom or how many times I could not remember because I did not know and I couldn't move. I was a mess and in pain—I was heartbroken and ashamed. I wanted to go home. Swede took me to the airport, dropped me at the curb with hardly a wave goodbye and my solitary journey began in earnest.

I became pregnant. I confirmed it at a clinic off campus in early March. The rabbit died. They really said that to me, and they seemed so happy for me; so many people wanted to adopt. I was horrified. I couldn't catch my breath. I didn't know what to do, but I didn't plan to tell my parents. They would be so disappointed in me. I was paralyzed with fear. What was there to do? I tried to talk about it with Swede. He never took nor returned any of my calls. When I finally made a decision, it was so late in the pregnancy.

I arranged an abortion through my roommate in Modesto. I took a Greyhound bus there and met the doctor in his office. I was five months pregnant, but had lied. It was a very difficult procedure. And I deserved every piercing bolt of pain. It was a healthy little boy. When the doctor was done and I could move, he took me back and deposited me at the bus station. He gave me a prescription for antibiotics, but I told him I didn't have any more money for medicine. He gave me $50 back and left me there and I waited for hours for the return bus to Davis. Instead, the good doctor came back. I thought that was so thoughtful, because I was in a great deal of pain, bleeding pretty badly and I was scared. He wanted to get me a room across the street where he would 'stay' with me and care for me. And I knew when he looked at me, how he intended to care for me and what I had become in his eyes. That was the beginning of my real education.

I waited for the bus and when it came, I felt like dying; I wanted to die. I had just murdered my little boy. I cried all the way back to campus on that Greyhound bus.

The next day, we had a softball game. I was the captain of our softball team and I had to play; I had to go. There was no way out. I was really sick, alone, in pain and afraid to play softball but I did for as long as I could. I think that is when I ruined myself, not that I didn't deserve it. I dropped out of college.

I was never able to have children. After having suffered painfully since I was in my early thirties, I had to have a full hysterectomy at 45, the final insult in my continuing punishment. I suffered horrid monthly agony. All of which was my fault and I deserved every bit of the torturous penalty.

My decline, my self-punishment and self-loathing continued. I thought, over time, I had worked myself into a sound place, with some measure of self-respect and with some level of confidence— finally. But each time, I would slip back into that dark abyss of the La Brea Tar Pits and choke on my guilt and recriminations until I could not function over twenty more years.

We all face decisions and they are neither right nor wrong. They are decisions hopefully made with the best of intentions at the time, albeit with an often heavy heart. Some decisions prove better than others, but there will always be the others. I did not want to be raped, but I made a bad decision that put me in harm's way. I made others that I regret, but there is no going back. So, it is for the decisions that have shaped me that I suffered, deservedly so. Those are the laws of man, the doctrines of my Church, and the teachings of my God. However, a small baby boy suffered more by my hand than I ever could, than he ever should. But, this is not a story of regret or condemnation. It is the story of life and the journey we all face alone, for awhile anyway. It is a story of forgiveness and hope: one that I feel I have finally earned. It is one that I hope I finally deserve.

I have made joyful decisions that have shaped me, too.

I married when I was almost thirty-six, a year after my mother died in my arms. I needed to love and be loved. I wanted happiness and forgiveness. My now husband was older than me by thirteen years with four grown children and custody of his youngest thirteen year old son. His son loved me almost immediately as only innocent children can do. They are healers, these small children so skillful at knitting broken lives together with love. We three married and vacationed in Niagara Falls where one of the most favorite photos of my life was taken.

When young Junior became a dating teen, I shared with him most of what had happened to me after I told his father. I didn't want either of them to know I was repeatedly raped because I did not deserve nor want their pity. I had lived with my horror for twenty years and bore the burden of my crime alone, as it should be. But, I wanted him to become a GOOD man, with respect for women and to take loving care of his partners and himself. I told him I decided to have an abortion, and as a Catholic, that had been a difficult decision for which I knew, and know to this day, I would burn in Hell. I didn't want him to make that same mistake and put himself or another young girl in such a position to face the same tortured decision. I wanted him to be a good person and a responsible lover. He cried, we all did, and he thanked me for telling him. He promised he would always do the right thing—and he has. He is a good person, a fine and honorable man.

I am proud he allows me to call him my son. He calls me Mumsie.

So, while the journey has been a long and difficult one for me, much good has come of it. I have a loving husband, a fulfilling life, a rewarding career and most importantly, I have raised a fine young man whom I dearly love and of whom I am extraordinarily proud. I have a son that loves me as his mother. He has enriched my life with every breath he takes, so much so that if I had to go through my worst nightmare all over again to arrive in the same place, I would.

He is the son I killed who has a redemption heart…and I am whole again.

Muffy Wilson

DEMON DEPRESSION

by

Teesa Mee

"I am me. That is the best I can be."

To all the people who struggle daily against depression, a silent killer, which needs our voices.

I have struggled with depression since I was a teen. In fact, in my adolescent years, I tried to take my life twice. I was diagnosed with fibromyalgia and rheumatoid arthritis at age 49 in 2003 and I was in the midst of a deep depression. Then in 2008, my 24-year-old son, who suffered with bipolar and borderline personality disorder, took his life. I did not want to live and many times considered following him. So how did I survive to the ripe old age of 61?

First, I surround myself with people who accept me as I am and give me self-confidence. These people include my husband of 36 years, my daughter, teachers, friends, and support groups.

Second, I participate in counseling. When my son began acting out in his early teens, I found a therapist to help me cope with his behaviors. However, during this counseling, my therapist also helped me to recognize the toxicity of my past. Don't give up if you cannot find a good therapist right out of the chute. I went through several over the years. I learned to view them as a tool. I may not have liked them, but they each offered me things to better my life.

Third, I use prescribed medication. I went on Paxil in my mid-thirties. PMS had gotten out of control and my depressive days were outnumbering my good days. It helped. I stayed on it for years and then weaned myself off. When I was in depression associated with fibro, I went on Cymbalta, which helped tremendously with fibro symptoms and depression. Medications don't always work first time either. Give each a fair shot. Ask for different ones if something is not working. Stand up for yourself. Depression and brain chemistry go together, just as diabetes and blood sugar chemistry do. You cannot always heal it on your own and you would not deprive your diabetic relative of insulin. Why deprive yourself of a chance to feel well by not taking antidepressants?

Fourth, I help boost my serotonin, the brain feel-good hormone, by eating dark chocolate. The darker the chocolate, the more helpful it is to serotonin levels. I love it bitter, 80% or higher chocolate content. However, since I recently gave up sugar, I have found cocoa nibs do the trick. As with any food item, moderation is the key. Just a square of dark chocolate a day seems to help.

Fifth, since I live in the northern tier of the USA, I am susceptible to S.A.D., seasonal affective disorder. My doctor prescribed Vitamin D, the sunshine vitamin, for me. Ask your doctor if you should be taking this supplement. I also invested in a light therapy lamp. There are several manufacturers such as Verilux. I sit with it shining in my eyes 30 minutes a day. It truly makes a difference in my mood during the grey winter months.

Sixth, I am good to myself by doing things I like such as reading and writing. Other options include dancing, singing, journaling, drawing, coloring, painting, sculpting, taking classes, walking, doing yoga, spending time with pets, and taking bubble baths. You matter! Don't let your bucket run dry by being there for everyone except yourself.

Seventh, I ask for lots of hugs. Go ahead! Ask the person sitting next to you for a hug, right now!

SUNSHINE

by

Teesa Mee

This poem is dedicated to my son, Nathan David, who died by suicide on 02-08-2008 at age 24. You are My Sunshine was one of our favorite lullabies and also a poem his birth mother included in things she sent to us when we adopted him. My apologies to the original lyricist.

Sunshine

You were my sunshine,
My firstborn sunshine.
You made me happy
And ended my grey days.
You'll never know, son,
How much I loved you,
Because you've taken your sunshine away.

The other night, son, when I lay sleeping
I dreamt I held you in my arms,
But when I woke, son,
I was mistaken
And I hung my head and cried.

You were my sunshine,
My firstborn sunshine.
You made me happy,
But now I'm grey.
You'll never know, son,
How much I loved you,
Because you've taken the sunshine away.

GRACE

by

Chelle Bliss

This is dedicated to my father.

The strongest man I know.

I love you, Dad.

Ataxia.

Life changer.

Destroyer of the strong.

Mobility snatcher.

Hated by many, known by few.

My father has always been my hero.

He still is.

He had that silent courage, wildly independent, stronger than Superman attitude that made people want to be around him.

There was never a moment he wasn't moving when I was a kid.

During the day, he worked his butt off at his home improvement business—building decks, installing hardwood floors, and taking old, dilapidated rooms and making them beautiful again. On the weekends, he worked on our house, always trying to make my mother happy.

I never once saw my father take a nap. His ass didn't ever hit the couch until at least ten at night. It wasn't in his nature. He had too much life to live.

About fifteen years ago, ataxia first started to affect my family. We didn't have a name for what was happening. We couldn't identify it as it snuck up in the shadows, lurking just out of sight, ready to steal away my father's independence and mobility without a warning.

I was on the brink of my first marriage. Yes, there's been more than one, but I remember it like it was yesterday. A week before the big day, my father broke the news that he received a ticket for drunk driving. To say we were shocked would be an understatement. He swore up and down that he'd only had two beers and he wasn't drunk at all. But the cop didn't believe him.

Months before, we'd started to notice that his speech had become slurred. My mother was quick to say it was his new dentures causing the speech problem, but I didn't buy it. When he was pulled over, not only was his speech slurred, but his coordination was impaired. The officer had no choice but to arrest him for DUI based on the field sobriety test. My father should've fought for a Breathalyzer, but he didn't.

I doubted my father's words for the first time in my life. He had to have drunk more than he admitted—a police officer wouldn't arrest him without cause.

Oh, how I was wrong.

Looking back on that event, I know it was the first stages of ataxia rearing its ugly head.

In time, people started to wonder if my father was an alcoholic. Little whispers at first, then phone calls came next. Every time, my mother would emphatically say "No!" Customers were concerned when he showed up in the morning with impaired speech. The first thing anyone thinks is alcohol. Eventually, my father's work started to slow down. A job that used to take him a week started to take two.

I begged him to go to the doctor. I knew something was wrong. But being the tough guy, he said no. He'd never been one to go to the doctor. He'd always been healthy. I can only remember one time in my first twenty years of life that my father spent a day in bed sick. Just one. He wasn't one to complain or dwell when something was wrong.

Later, he admitted that he worried he may have had a stroke. That was the only thing that made sense. When he confided in me about his fears of a stroke, I remember being scared. God, what would I do without my father? What if he had another stroke, but he didn't survive the next time?

Skip ahead a few years. Eventually, he grew too weak to work. After a discussion, my parents decided to move to Florida to be closer to me. I started researching his symptoms and was finally able to convince him to go to a doctor.

Victory.

They'd fix him.

Wrong.

Shortly after my parents settled into their new life in Florida, I took my dad for his first checkup since he left the navy some thirty years before. The general physician referred my father to a neurologist and handed us a piece of paper to give to the doctor during our visit.

That piece of paper changed our lives forever.

We had a name for it.

Ataxia.

That night I went home and searched the Internet, needing to find out everything I could. Was it curable? Would it continue? What would happen to my dad? I learned so much about ataxia that my head was spinning.

No longer was "stroke" the scariest word I'd ever heard. Ataxia had taken its place.

There were so many variations of ataxia. Some genetic. Some environmental.

But most important and soul crushing—all degenerative.

Incurable and untreatable were the two words that stuck out the most to me.

That's not what I'd hoped to find out in my research.

I thought I could still save the day.

My father would be different.

I could change his fate.

There was a small glimmer of hope when I found that the University of South Florida had an Ataxia Research Center. How lucky were we? Six years ago, there weren't many, but here was one practically in our backyard.

We sat for hours in the waiting room, ready to hear that there was some miracle cure that hadn't been published yet. To say I was anxious was an understatement. I blamed myself for this. My father hadn't had a name for it, hadn't had the fear that his life was about to change with no hope in sight, but I gave him that reality. I made him go to the doctor.

By the time we left after meeting with the one of the best ataxia doctors in the country, I didn't have any more hope than I did when we walked through the door. She told us that it was important to determine what type of ataxia my father suffered from to determine a course of action. By that, she meant physical therapy and to figure out how long he'd be able to continue to walk without assistance.

My father started to undergo tests, wanting to find out what caused his ataxia. My father's father's family didn't have a trace of it. His mother's family we had no information about. My father had been abandoned as a baby by his mother and never knew that side of his family. I, being the history geek that I am, searched the Internet and finally found a few relatives living in New Jersey. They assured me that they'd never heard of it or had any memories of anyone suffering from it in the family.

It seemed like maybe there was something in his past causing it.

He did every blood test, had an MRI, CAT scan, and still nothing pointed to a reason why he was suffering and continuing to get worse.

His doctor then ordered a genetic test. Even with no traces of it in the family, maybe the right combination of genes hadn't occurred until his birth. I don't know to this day how my father felt about having a genetic test, but I know it scared the holy shit out of me.

I mean… he's *my* dad.

If he has a genetic form, there's a high chance I do too.

Did I want to know if I'd be plagued by the same thing in a few decades? Is it better to know that something bad is going to happen?

I know people like to say, "Well, you can plan for it, at least." I don't want to plan for it. I don't want the knowledge to be hanging over my head and always in the back of my mind. Even if he did have a genetic form of ataxia, it wasn't a given that I did too. Either way, we went forward with the testing. The doctor warned us it was expensive, but my father was fully covered by Blue Cross Blue Shield, just like he had been for the last thirty years.

But—and this is a huge but—BCBS, being the amazingly shit-tastic insurance company that they are, denied the test. Yes, you read that right. They DENIED it. They said there was too little known about the genetic test and the validity of the results.

I was beside myself. I didn't want to know the results, but if there was one way to know if there was any possible treatment for my father, this test was it.

That viperous, life-sucking insurance company took that from me. From us.

Over thirty years of premiums without having to pay a claim on my father earned him nothing. They'd made a killing on him for years. The one time we needed them, they turned their backs.

My father never went back to the ataxia specialist after that. What was the point? There was no cure. She couldn't pinpoint what caused his symptoms. I couldn't convince him to go back. I don't blame my dad. The constantly poke and prod you to get more information. That's great if there's hope after learning the results they're seeking. But when there's nothing that can be done, why cause more suffering?

Today, my father can walk short distances without any assistance, but he opts for a walker to help him keep his stability. He tried to explain to me what it's like to live with ataxia.

"See that spot on the ground?" he asked, pointing to a dark splotch on the cement.

Yeah."

"If your brain tells your foot to touch it, your foot will. But when I do the same, my foot goes everywhere but that spot."

Not only has it robbed him of his ability to talk without getting frustrated by other people's inability to understand, but it's robbed him of so much more. He can barely write anymore; it looks all jagged and like chicken scratch. He can't do the simplest tasks without a lot of determination and energy.

My father, the one who could build an addition to a house like it was nothing, can no longer use a hammer. The very thought of it brings tears to my eyes.

Watching my superhero deteriorate before my eyes has been one of the most painful things in my life. No matter how wealthy I become or what I do, I'll never be able to fix him.

Some things money can't buy. Health is one of them.

My father doesn't complain about his life, although he has every reason to do so. He always says, "Shit happens" and "It is what it is."

I want to rescue him and make him better. Our parents raise us and give us, if we're lucky, everything we need to be successful and healthy for the rest of our lives. I want to do that for him. I want to heal him. Shit, at this point, I'd love to be able just to lessen his symptoms, but I know there's nothing I can do.

I'm helpless.

It's not a feeling I know well. I've always been the one to figure shit out and come out on top.

Always.

It was something my parents taught me. I'm independent because of them. I've never had to rely on someone else for my existence. But no matter what I do, I'm still *helpless* when it comes to ataxia and my father.

At Christmas, I bought my father an iPad so he can text members of the family and his friends. Cell phones are too small and the buttons too puny that he'd never be able to type a message. We text every day, and I cherish each conversation I have with my dad. I don't take him for granted. Each day with him is precious.

He's still my go-to person for advice. He's never led me wrong. Usually, he tells me to follow what I know is right. He always gave me enough room to make the wrong decision and never once said "I told you so" when I failed. As far as fathers go, I won the freaking lottery the day I was born.

I'm crying as I type this. Knowing someday I'll be without this man is something I can't comprehend. Even with his suffering each day, I never want to let go.

I don't know who I am without him.

I only hope that, if I'm faced with the same fate, I'll do it with as much grace and dignity as my father has shown the last fifteen years.

Dad,

You're my hero.

My first love.

My forever.

You've left a permanent imprint on my life.

Thank you for making me the way I am.

I love you, Daddy.

Always & Forever,

Chelle

EMBRACE

by

Komal Chandwani

"It is often in the darkest skies that we see the brightest stars."

- Richard Evans

To mom, dad, and grandparents.

Thank you for being there to guide me when I took every small step to a huge challenge.

Thank you for being there when I needed you.

Chapter One

"I feel my heart ache, but I've forgotten what that feeling means."

- Chuck Palahniuk

Imogen Greene

The monotonous beeping sounds of the machines gave me a headache, as I stood in the hospital room looking down at my grandmother. She had been admitted to the hospital after fainting a couple of hours ago and hadn't woken up yet. The cause was still unknown; the doctors took some blood samples for tests and walked away, no one was telling me anything. They explained to me that my grandma was old and that these things happened. I understood that, but fainting the way she did and not waking up? That was definitely unusual and needless to say, I was worried.

This incident occurred around ten last night when I had just returned home from a friend's house party. The lights were off, which was strange because grandma always kept them on. I'd called out to her several times but was only greeted by silence.

The upstairs rooms were empty so I'd quickly run down the stairs. My eyes peeped into the kitchen and that's when I saw her, lying motionlessly on the floor.

The high I was on washed away as fear set in my bones and all the blood drained from my face. Dread came over me and guilt settled in for going out. If I had stayed home as grandma had instructed, maybe this wouldn't have happened.

I'd rushed towards her, picked up her head, and placed it on my lap. Her cold skin sent shivers down my spine and my body shook with terror at the thought of losing my grandmother. With trembling fingers, I'd grabbed a glass of water and sprinkled some of it on her face.

There wasn't even a slightest movement in her body. I remember letting out a garbled grunt of frustration. My heart thrashed against my ribcage and everything in my surroundings faded away until all I could hear was my beating heart.

Time froze in that moment and there was only one thought that played in my mind.

I cannot lose her, she is my only family.

I cannot lose her…

In my messed up state, reality somehow caught up and slapped me back to my senses. If it hadn't been for the vibration of my phone, I would have sat there glued to that spot for God knows how long. I quickly called 911 and hoped they would come as soon as possible.

Holding up and remaining calm was essential; my grandma's safety was priority.

***

Tears threatened to spill. My body slumped down on the visitor's chair. My hands covered my face. My elbows dug into my thighs. I took a deep breath in an attempt to calm my thumping heart. It felt like it was going to jump out of my chest. It hurt so much. I didn't know how to drive away this feeling. Gulping down the lump that formed at the back of my throat, I squeezed my eyes shut.

What will I do if she leaves me?

My mind started to take me to dark places on its own accord. I couldn't stop it from pulling me into my past as I took a trip down memory lane.

Six years ago. I can never forget what happened that night. It's as if it happened only yesterday. The knot in my stomach grew as flashes of that horrible night appeared.

The screeching of car tires made my head pound so hard that I wanted to scream. I could see my dad driving the car while mom was sitting beside him. He took a sharp turn to...to save...

The sudden placement of a hand on my shoulder startled me. As a reflex, my feet slam to the ground, causing the chair to topple over. My hands grabbed my chest at a last ditched attempt to calm my alarmed self.

Flashbacks had always been exhausting and, at times they'd triggered panic attacks but this time, thankfully, there were none.

"I am so sorry, please forgive me. I didn't mean to startle you," the doctor in front of me gushed as he kneeled down to pick up the chair.

"Doctor Cooper?"

He brushed his unkempt hair from his forehead and straightened up as he looked at me; it was indeed Dr. Cooper. His clothes were disheveled and I wondered what he was doing here at two in the morning.

I stared at him in disbelief, trying to catch my breath. His presence could only mean bad news.

"Hey, let's talk," he said, as he nervously motioned his hands towards the door and gave a side glance towards grandma.

Dr. Lance Cooper had always been of the shy type. It was quite hard to comprehend considering he was a psychiatrist. Even though he got all squirmy, if you stared at him for long, he was damn good at his job. I've heard people say it was easy to warm up to him but I never felt that when we had sessions together.

After my parents had passed, it was mandatory for me to visit a psychiatrist, though Granny thought the same since I had stopped talking to everyone and slowly pushed them away. When I started being distant from Granny too, she got worried and told this to Dr. Cooper. Since then, he had been calling me quite frequently for sessions.

Just the thought of my parents squeezed my heart. The memory to date caused pain, a pain that I had not yet shared with anyone. I couldn't, it was difficult to think of them while descending into a fragile state.

Pushing those thoughts away, I concentrated on the present, turned, and gave Granny one last look before nodding at Dr. Cooper. He opened the door and closed it behind him once we were standing in the hall.

My eyes searched his face for a tell but it remained blank.

"Imogen, please sit."

My head shook. "No, not until you tell me what's wrong!"

"Imogen, please. You-"

"Just tell me what it is, Dr. Cooper. I am not a kid anymore and can handle what you have to say," I kept my voice firm while talking.

The look on his face was not good. He sighed and ran his fingers through his blonde hair and those blue eyes of his locked with my brown ones. He was serious when he told me to sit down. I should have listened because what he was about to say made my world crumble.

"Your grandma's condition doesn't look too good. She is too weak to go on. The doctors are still conducting tests, but I wanted to make sure you are prepared for whatever happens."

"No…this cannot be happening again," I whispered to myself.

My knees gave way, but Dr. Cooper was there to hold me. He helped me to one of the benches and made me sit. He was there by my side until I could no longer take it. The only person keeping me going was my grandma; she was all I had.

I didn't realize tears were wildly falling from my eyes until Dr. Cooper handed me a handkerchief. I murmured a thank you but looked away.

Why was life so hard? Why couldn't anything nice happen when I needed it the most?

"Imogen, I'd like to have a session with you tomorrow. It is advisable that you come in. I know this time is hard, and you think life is unfair, but you need to be strong, okay? For your grandma."

"Okay," I nodded, subconsciously agreeing to have a session with him.

I didn't know how it would be for me tomorrow, since I never really spoke to him about most of my feelings. I wasn't sure if I was ready to talk to him about Granny, and especially not about what happened six years ago.

Chapter Two

"I'm not sure this is a world I belong in anymore. I'm not sure that I want to wake up."

- Gayle Forman

Dr. Cooper had forced me to go home last night. I was reluctant at first because leaving grandma alone like that didn't sit well with me, but he assured me time and again that the hospital staff would take good care of her, and that I needn't worry about her.

With a heavy heart, I had left the hospital in hopes that my grandmother would be alright. When I got home, all I could think about was how I'd found my grandmother's cold, barely alive body on the kitchen floor.

The flashbacks almost triggered a panic attack but somehow I was able to take control of it. I took deep breaths as Dr. Cooper had taught me and though the aftershocks still made my body tremble, my legs took me to my room without stumbling and I got into bed with my clothes still on. The entire night I tossed and turned and when I couldn't take it anymore, I went for an early jog. Skipping breakfast and eager to meet Granny, I left home at eight.

When I arrived at the hospital, the clinical smell hit my nostrils, creating a burning sensation, and I scowled. This smell always made me feel nauseated and reminded me of what I went through six years ago today. Being here on this day was a bold move for me. Even if I wanted to curl up and stay in bed, I couldn't. My grandma needed me today and abandoning her in this situation, when she helped me these years, would be inconsiderate.

Walking towards the elevator, I passed through the emergency ward and saw a few patients waiting outside. My gaze fell upon a little girl who sat on one of the benches. Her head hung low and by the looks of her, it seemed as if she had been crying for a while now. I stopped in my tracks and made my way towards her. She reminded me of myself when I sat in the same exact spot *that* night. I was so lost then, that I had given up on life.

I looked around and found no one besides the girl. Frowning, I crouched down and gently placed my hand on her knee. My gesture startled her and she backed away further into her seat.

"Hey, don't be scared, okay? My name is Imogen. What's your name?"

I spoke to her as calmly as I could; I didn't want to scare her any more than she already was. Striking up a small conversation and maybe distracting her would be a good thing, or so I thought. Kids got distracted easily, didn't they?

Shifting from my position and standing up, I shuffled to the seat beside her. Facing her, I took a minute to take in her current state. Her blonde hair was completely disheveled and smeared with mud and her blue dress was torn in places, though it appeared to be keeping her warm.

When she looked up at me, her hazel eyes glistened with tears and you could see that some had already left their trail on her cheeks. She was beyond terrified with whatever situation she was in. *What could've possibly happened to leave this little girl so lost?*

My heart went out to her. I once again tried talking to her hoping that this time she would talk to me. "Where are your parents, honey?"

At the mention of her parents, her lips visibly trembled and she started sobbing. Big fat tears roll down her cheeks and I just wanted to hug her.

Minutes passed by and her sobs turned into cries. The people sitting in the waiting room stared at us and started whispering to one another. I started to get all squirmy. Being in the spotlight never sat well with me and having their gazes directed towards me made me want to hide.

I began to get nervous with each passing second; I didn't know how to handle this, maybe I should have just walked past her. All those thoughts vanished as I peered down at her. Before taking her little hand in my big one, I thought about it for several minutes. I had no clue how she'd react to my touch this time. When I cautiously placed my hand above hers, she surprisingly didn't flinch from the touch. Instead, she held onto it and after a while, pulled me down to her level. I wondered what she was doing but she only pulled me closer so that she could wrap her arms around my neck.

I was taken aback by her gesture. Warmth and empathy filled my heart as I picked her up and placed her little body on my lap. Wrapping my arms around her, I made sure that she felt safe.

She hugged me tightly and cried into my chest. I swallowed my tears and tried to soothe her by trying to talk to her. It all reminded me of my past, how scared I was back then.

"Mommy told me that she would come back…" she tried to speak in between her sobs. Her chest heaved as the little girl gasped for air.

"Your mom-"

"How many times have I told you to stay put and not bother the people around you?!"

Before I even had the chance to finish my sentence, a nurse came by and took the girl from my arms. The girl struggled against the nurse's hold and tried to grab my hand but the nurse only pulled her further away from me.

Anger filled me and I quickly stood up, taking a menacing step towards the nurse, I warned her.

"Let the girl go. This is no way to treat a child!"

My voice grew in octaves and I didn't care what the people around me thought. The nurse's actions were rough and could've caused pain to the girl. How dare she!

"I am sorry miss, but I'll have to take her now. Thea's parents-"

"You know, I don't give a damn about your reason. Let the child go now, apologize to her, and we'll be good. Otherwise, I'll be forced to write a complaint against you to the Dean and that will be your ticket out of this hospital!"

Thea flailed her arms and tried to break free. Seeing her like that only increased my concern for her. I glared at the nurse and her body visibly stiffened. Satisfied with the reaction, I grabbed the nurse's hand and helped Thea out of her hold.

"Thea, that's a pretty name," I whispered, scooping up the little girl in my arms.

She buried her face in the crook of my neck and hugged me tightly. Her grip was strong enough to choke me, but I didn't say anything, it was alright, I could handle it.

"Ma'am, please…," the nurse's voice was laced with urgency and that got my attention. I know I went a bit far with my temper but she was wrong on her part.

My lips formed a hard line and I gave her a nod.

"Thea's parents have been in an accident and sadly, they didn't make it. We had to call Child Protective Services," she explained, pleading with her eyes.

I swallowed the lump that had formed in the back of my throat. It was happening all over again. Thea's situation was reflecting my own past and I couldn't take it. Today, six years ago, I had lost my parents in an accident as well and hearing about this girl's parents only worsened my condition. It was too much to take in.

Thea needed someone to be at her side, someone strong, but she was all alone. The question was, could I be strong enough for this little girl until her relatives arrived?

I frowned. "Why the Child Protective Services though? Didn't you call her relatives? And-"

The conversation was cut short when Dr. Cooper stepped in. I hadn't even realized that he was standing in the same room.

"Imogen, can I have a word with you?"

I pursed my lips and nodded. I walked towards him with Thea in my arms, but he shook his head at the kid. Getting the message and gently placing her on her feet, I turned away, but she stopped me by tugging my hoodie.

"Hey, kid. Stay here for a minute, okay? I'll be right back." I kissed her forehead.

Thea blinked several times before carefully nodding at me.

"Yes?"

"Why are you creating a fuss so early this morning?"

"Sue me for helping out a kid who is being treated disrespectfully, Dr. Cooper!" I scoffed.

"Call me Lance, please. Listen, Imogen, please calm down. I am sure we can talk calmly and figure something out, okay?" he requested.

Ignoring Dr. Cooper, I looked back at Thea and the nurse. Something had been bothering me since she'd stepped into my personal space, taking Thea away.

"Why did the hospital have to call Child Protective Services, *Lance*?" I whispered, but made sure to speak his name coldly.

Dr. Cooper heard me and sighed as he stood behind me. I bent down and held Thea's hand. Looking up, I glared at the nurse, again. She seemed worried and looked anywhere but at me.

Lance cleared his throat and motioned for us to follow him. The nurse gave me a stink eye before following him to his office. I shrugged, shook my head, and followed suit.

Chapter Three

"The journey of a thousand miles begins with one step."

- Lao Tzu

I stared at *Lance* in disbelief. He let the nurse just walk right out of his office without even telling her anything. He did not even speak a word to her about whatever happened back there.

Thea now sat on one of the couches besides me; she looked so shaken by the entire situation. Explaining to her that her parents were dead was going to be a difficult task. Plus, why would the hospital simply want to shrug off the responsibility of calling her relatives? How much could this little girl take before the entire situation broke her completely?

"Imogen, you know you have to talk to me at some point. Tell me what is on your mind," he spoke as if nothing had happened. The calm in his voice irked me and made my eye twitch.

"You really want to know what's wrong? This little girl," I got up and pointed my finger towards Thea; "she just lost her parents. So help me understand why her relatives haven't been called and why there was no one taking care of her outside."

Even though I was furious, I had to be as calm as I could for the kid. I had to put my anger on a leash because I didn't want to scare Thea. If she thought she could trust me, I wanted to keep it that way.

"I want you to sit down and take a deep breath. If you are not calm, we cannot proceed. I will call one of nurses and have them take care of Thea until our session is over. Trust me on this, okay?"

He searched my face for confirmation. When I didn't say anything, he sighed and pressed his lips into a hard line. I knew I was being difficult but could you blame me after what just happened?

Finally, I gave in and curtly nodded at him. He got up from across me and went to his desk. Pressing the intercom button, he waited until someone knocked on the door. When a nurse stepped into the room, Dr. Cooper walked towards Thea, bent down to her eye level and with a gentle voice, instructed her to go with the nurse.

She looked at me with confusion so I gave her a nod and an assuring smile that meant it was alright for her to go. Thea jumped off the couch and stalked over to where the nurse stood, but not before giving me a kiss on the cheek. To be honest, I was taken aback by her gesture.

However, that was the first time in years I had genuinely smiled, and for a moment, I felt at peace. Seeing the little girl look up to me was something I'd never imagined.

I kept looking at Thea until her brown curly hair got lost in the corridor and the door was closed shut.

The room had gone silent and the thickness of tension had increased, I turned towards him only to catch him staring at me. I cleared my throat and hoped that I could convey my true emotions.

Before I could get on with what I had to say, Dr. Cooper halted me. He raised his index finger, pushed himself off of his desk, and sat from across me.

"I know you are ready to talk, Imogen," he said, "but I want you to take baby steps. Tell me what your concern is regarding Thea."

I placed both of my hands on my lap and stared at them. I couldn't look him in the eye and talk. If I did, I wouldn't be able to convey what I had to say properly. It had always been difficult for me to talk to a psychiatrist. It wasn't just him. Shrinks scared the crap out of me.

I mentally shook my head. I was getting distracted again and now wasn't the time to drift away; I had to open to someone someday.

I walked Dr. Cooper through the events of the morning and tried to tell him how exactly I felt about Thea's situation. All the time that I spoke, he did not interrupt me, neither did he give me any judgmental eyes.

The pain and irritation that I felt started to slowly fade away. The unease I'd been feeling subsided as minutes passed. I naturally warmed up to Dr. Cooper because I spoke to him without any hesitation. I still couldn't look him in the eye at the end of what I had to say, but I felt confident about talking to him.

He smiled at me, a genuine smile and gave me a nod, which meant I did well and deep down, I felt proud of myself.

"Clearing up all the confusion regarding Thea - she doesn't have any living relatives. Her grandparents from her father's side have passed away, while the ones from her mother's side said they want nothing to do with her."

"And how do you know about this?" I challenged, not believing a word he said.

"I have been in contact with Thea's family before. That's all I can give you. No more than that because I do not have the privilege to do so," a look of sympathy was what he gave me.

The poor confused soul might be looking for answers and there was no one who could provide them to her. How do you explain to a little girl that she was never going to see her mother again? How could her grandparents be so inconsiderate?! Their grandchild needed them. I remembered when Granny had taken me in and consoled me when my parents had passed away. At least I had someone by my side.

There might be several questions at the tip of her tongue but how was she supposed to convey her thoughts? Everyone around here was so intimidating and cold; Thea needed someone whom she could warm up to and help her.

"How old is she?" I asked Dr. Cooper.

"Four."

My eyes widened in consternation.

"What?" I screeched! "That poor girl."

"You don't need to worry about her, Imogen."

I laughed humorlessly. "Are you kidding me, doc? You know what happens to kids who go into foster care. You know the system is broke."

"What do you want then?"

My eyebrows rose, taken aback by his question. *What did I want?*

"I want Thea to be safe and I want to make sure that she is properly taken care of."

"Does that mean you want to keep in contact with the little girl in the future?"

I wasn't sure where this conversation was heading but I nodded my head in confirmation.

"Then you know what you have to do. You need to be strong around her, can you do that, Imogen?"

"Yes. Yes, I can try."

"You will have to let go of your troubles because Thea's life is never going to be the same and helping her cope will be difficult. She will have psychiatric assistance like you did, but we don't know how that will turn out." Dr. Cooper spoke the truth.

I closed my eyes and took a deep breath. I knew I had to face Dr. Cooper and his questions, I couldn't run away from this forever. I had to be bold and take a step forward, not backwards. Did I have it in me to look upon my past and embrace it? Was I ready to talk about what happened six years ago? I knew that was the only thing holding me back.

For years I had denied whatever happened the night of accident. My nature of pushing that away lay heavily on my shoulders, and I didn't want that for Thea. I may not know her personally, but she was an innocent soul who had a long way to go, and I would do anything to protect her from making the same mistakes I did.

The darkness that I thought I was living in wasn't dark after all. My grandmother was always by my side and she never left, no matter what. She supported me in all ways possible and she took me in when there was no one else. She raised me all by herself, helped me through school and, despite her sickness, she even made it to my graduation ceremony. Deep down, I felt proud because I made her happy but I seemed to have overlooked that happy moment because something else was standing in my way. Something that I should've spoken about a lot sooner.

I inhaled a good amount of air and exhale through my lips. When I thought I was calm enough to talk, I locked my gaze with Dr. Cooper.

"I am ready to talk about what happened six years ago."

Chapter Four

"You wake up every morning to fight the same demons that left you so tired the night before, and that, my love, is bravery."

- Anonymous

"Let's start this from the beginning, okay? Baby steps," Lance told me as he kept his notepad aside.

"Okay."

"Tell me what you were doing the night of your parents' accident."

My heart rate accelerated at the mention of my parents and their accident but I kept silently chanting that I could do it. Even for a moment when I thought I couldn't speak, Thea's lost face flashed before my eyes and that was what kept me going.

"I was at a sleepover party when a huge fight occurred due to a misunderstanding. I didn't know what to do. My friend Lacey had invited her boyfriend over and I was surprised because her parents were conservative, but later I came to know that the guy had snuck in. He didn't come alone either, he'd brought along a couple of friends. I just didn't feel comfortable. I walked down the stairs to the kitchen and I could feel this guy Shaun's eyes on me. He was way too old for us and he didn't seem like a decent guy.

I was scared. As I walked by him, he grabbed my hips, turned me around, and kissed me. He forced that kiss on me and the only thing I could do was struggle against his hold.

Somehow I managed to push him away and he stumbled down the stairs and he fell pretty hard. That was it, the moment when time seemed to slip from my fingers."

I hadn't realized that I was crying until Lance handed me a handkerchief. I dabbed my eyes but kept going. I needed to get this out.

"What happened next, Imogen?"

"He created a ruckus and that awakened Lacey's parents. They were so shocked, then they started yelling at her and everything got pretty messed up. When I explained to them what had happened, they threatened to call the cops on the guys, so they quickly left, but not before throwing a warning glare at me.

Lacey was pissed with what I had done. I thought she would be concerned about me or at least be on my side but she was unhappy that my 'stupid attention grabbing stunt' cost her time with her boyfriend.

I couldn't stay there anymore so I-I called my parents and left."

Tears streamed down my face as I began to recollect my parents' face. The way mom looked at me through the car window, she must have been so worried.

"Lacey came out and started another fight with me on the sidewalk, she even slapped me. Funny, I used to call her a friend. Then our fight got pretty nasty; her hands were all over me and she was really mad because her parents were grounding her until graduation.

In the moment, I didn't know what to do, so I pushed her away from me; she fell on the road just when my parents' drove in. To save her, dad took a sharp turn; the car skidded along the ice clad road and turned upside down. I ran towards them and screamed for them but the car had caught fire before I could even make it. It was all my fault."

***

It had been a year since I met Thea in the hospital. That day held a significant place in my life, seven years ago and even now. I may have lost my parents then but I'd gained my grandma, who'd guided me and taken care of me till her last dying breath.

Meeting Thea had been my defining moment. This little girl made me realize in six hours what I couldn't learn and embrace in six years. When I'd put myself in Thea's shoes, my past had flashed in front of my eyes, making me realize what I had done...or not done.

Thea lost her parents and when her grandparents didn't take her in, I did. I took her in my arms and made her a promise that day, to take care of her and be by her side, always. Lance had to clear me out first before I filled the forms for Thea's custody. I felt much better when I spoke to him about what had happened.

That day Lance had canceled all his appointments just for me. He stayed with me, consoled me, and made me feel better. Six years of misery had caused me so much pain. All those years I had blamed myself, but Lance showed me that it wasn't my fault. It was life and we had to accept whatever reality threw in our way. He told me that the memory would never fade, that it would always stay with me, but I had to find a way to embrace it and move on.

Since then, I had been having regular sessions with him and I was getting better. I hadn't realized how much Lance had helped me cope, not just during his sessions, but also when he was off the clock.

One day I was picking up some books for Thea when I bumped into him. It was roughly six months after when I got cleared up. Lance told me that I was good to go on my own, that I could attend sessions when I needed them, and that they were no longer mandatory.

That day he asked me out on a coffee. After that it began to be a usual thing, going out somewhere where I could freely talk to him.

The intimidating office of his wasn't there to bother me and I felt good.

Lance was a really nice guy. Time passed by and our casual meetings turned into something more. I was reluctant at first because in my twenty one years of existence, I had never dated anyone, but I didn't want to hold back anymore, so when he proposed to me, I said yes.

We were taking things slowly; the good part about all of this was that Granny would have approved of him and Thea loved him dearly.

"Gen-gen! Look whose here!!" Thea's voice pulled me out of my stupor as she came running towards me.

Her little body crashed into my legs and she giggled. Tugging at my top she pulled me down.

"What's up, cupcake?" I smiled.

"Lance is here!" she excitedly announced.

Lance came into the kitchen and picked Thea up into his arms. She cackled as she kissed him on the cheek. Lance blew raspberries on her stomach and she broke into a fit of giggles.

I smiled at both of them. Lance caught me staring at them and smirked. *Cocky.*

My life had taken a complete turnaround. I never imagined I'd ever be content with my life, but now I was, thanks to the people in my life.

Lance whispered something to Thea and she ran off towards the dining room.

He never took his eyes off of me; he came forward and kissed me deeply and I sighed, content. This was where I belonged.

It took me six years to realize and accept my parents' death. Oddly, I was glad that it took me so many years; had the realization hit me before, I wouldn't have met an amazing little girl and a loving boyfriend.

Whatever has to happen will happen and it will happen at the right time.

ONE MOMENT

by

JP Barry

"She made broken look beautiful and strong look invincible. She walked with the Universe on her shoulders and made it look like a pair of wings."

- Ariana

To Eugene, Anita & Leslie – Three of the greatest gifts the Universe could've ever given me.

To my Muse – Everything limitless.

The tag line for THE NEARER THE DAWN is, 'One moment can change everything.' While coming up with this, of course, the words meant something but, to be honest, they didn't really strike a chord until recently. However, they fit the manuscript perfectly, so a tagline was born.

Over the course of my life, I've experienced many 'one moment' life changes. Some were good, some were bad, but others were epic. The sad part is, we don't realize the extent and effect of these memories until after the moment has passed. When you remember these lost moments, however, you can turn it into something amazing.

I'm a fairly private person; there is the work version and the non-work version of me. I've never had a problem being the work version, but rarely do I open up and share my personal life. Hey, it's called a personal life for a reason, right?

A while ago someone challenged me to open up and be myself. The sheer thought of this vulnerable exposure was enough to make my palms sweaty and butt squirm in the chair. To this person, who will remain nameless, my actions were intriguing and entertaining enough that they continued to push my limits. After a few hours of them asking questions and me talking myself in comfortable circles, I finally gave up and gave in because I was fighting a losing battle.

Purging the good, bad, and epic memories was by far the most cathartic experience of my life. Yes, there were times when I wanted to stop talking, times when I found myself smiling like a fool, times when I had to hold back tears, and times when I wanted to book it out of the coffeehouse and run far, far away, never to return.

However, when it was over there was clarity. The frustrations and fears I had been clinging to so desperately were gone. I had relived all of the 'one moments' which had made me the emotional train wreck sitting there that day.

Initially, I felt the weight I'd been carrying around lift off my shoulders and it felt good. Truthfully, it felt amazing to be exposed and vulnerable for once. I found myself wondering why I never tried this before. While parting ways with this person, they selflessly provided me with yet another 'one moment,' as assurance they had not judged me for what I had said. Being lost in that moment with this person felt as if I had been found for the first time.

It took a while before the true effect of what they'd done for me kicked in. The result? The Muse I thought I'd lost returned and my characters awoke. The words my fingers were typing on the pages of my manuscripts were much more powerful, passionate, and meaningful. All those little defining 'one moments' gave me back the power I had lost.

Now I realize this person will not read this, even though a lifelong bond was created that day, but if by some twist of fate they do come across this, thank you. You'll never know how much you've done for me and because of that, how much you mean to me. I could go on, but I'll leave it at that, you know who you are.

One moment *can* change everything. Add up all the 'one moments' and they will equal something amazing and strong. Challenge yourself to let down your walls and experience exposure and vulnerability. You just might find peace and clarity like I have.

We are all battling something, whether it be an internal or external issue is not important. What is important is there is safety in numbers, which means you are not alone. The Universe is always at work and will send you what you need. Before my nameless person came into my life, I had spent many nights crying and telling myself to be strong. Forcing myself to believe things would get better when my mind was filled with doubt and the need to fake being okay when

I wasn't. My nameless person saw through that; they were my gift from the Universe. Now, I challenge all of you to listen to what the Universe is whispering; embrace it and you will find the peace and calmness you'll need when trying to endure life's roughest storms.

BREAKING THE STEPS

by

A.M. Wilson

"You may not control all the events that happen to you, but you can decide not to be reduced by them."

- Maya Angelou. *Letter to My Daughter, a book of essays* (2009)

To anyone who feels like they can't breathe deep enough

That the world isn't bright enough

That they can't get warm enough,

This is for you.

Fighting depression is like running on the treadmill while everybody else is running along the street. Your lungs burn. Your legs scream in agony, begging you to stop. They tire easily, and you want to get off.

You want to get off.

God, you want to get off.

People run past. They run—almost as if they fly.

Some jog. Some even walk.

They use minimal effort to get their tasks done. They do the dishes and clean the house. Pack up their six kids and their dog then head to work and the park, the movies, baseball practice and gymnastics. Then everyone comes back home for family movie night, and they're all so happy.

And you're still at that sink.

Your elbows rest on the edge, and your shoulders are slumped. Your back hunches in defeat. Your shoulders shake as you try to hold back the anguished sobs rising in your throat. Because it hurts. It feels like physical pain trying to complete that task they find so simple. You don't understand why you have to struggle. Why you're stuck running in place while the rest of the world flies past with ease. You don't understand why it's so hard for you.

You pick up the next dish.

Because you do have pride. And you have people who are watching, so your problems you try desperately to hide.

Those dishes take three times the effort, and the next task takes four.

And so on and so forth, until by the time you're dressed and ready for the day you just want to crawl back into bed.

You don't.

You keep on. You push. You fight, because you're strong, even though you feel weak. Possibly even the weakest you've ever been. You keep on, because it's what you were made to do.

To persevere.

To push forward.

The moment you want to give up is when you push harder than you ever have. The pinnacle of failure is also the foundation of victory.

You can't give up.

You won't.

You'll fight. You'll drag on. Not really for yourself, or so it feels, but because people are depending on you. Your boss. Your children. Your significant other. Your parents.

You carry forth, and put one foot in front of the other on that belt. Day after day. Week after week. Month after month.

One day, you'll look around you.

You'll wonder where all the time has gone. Winter has turned into summer. Piles of dirty snow have melted into fresh puddles after a sun shower. Blankets of pure white are now woven fields of green. You'll want to feel the sun.

The challenge lies before you, but instead of feeling afraid, you feel empowered. Enough of this monotony.

Your legs slow to a jog, to a walk. And for the first time in days, weeks, months, years even, you take a step off that treadmill. You step onto the solid ground.

All the time spent fighting, pushing, climbing the simplest tasks that felt mountainous, you were getting stronger. Your body was getting stronger. Those first steps feel like you could tackle the world.

Fighting depression is like running on the treadmill while everybody else is running along the street. But when you finally find the courage to step off, you'll realize you are strong.

THIS BEAUTIFUL ESCAPE

by

Heather Dahlgren

"Courage is not having the strength to go; it is going on when you don't have the strength."

- Theodore Roosevelt

To everyone who has found the courage to keep going. You are not alone.

We all at some point in our lives are faced with situations where we need to find the courage to keep going. Whether it is illness, loss or everyday stress, sometimes we simply need someone to tell us it is going to be alright. We need to know we are not alone.

You may have been diagnosed with an illness that is going to take a great battle. You may need to fight harder than you've had to before, that's when you grab onto that courage. I have fibromyalgia. I have days were I can't touch my own skin without crying in pain. I have days where standing, sitting, laying, all hurt. I have learned my triggers and if I can avoid them I do. Sometimes that is impossible with life, but I will never stop living. I know the battle of fighting for your health. You can do this, you are not alone. You are going to be alright.

You may have lost someone you love. You may feel like your world is crumbling around you, that you will never be the same. That's when you need to find your courage and hold on tight. I have suffered great loss in my life starting at a young age. I have lost all my grandparents, my sister and both of my parents. When I recently lost my dad, I didn't know what I was going to do. I lost my mom when I was young and my dad was my world. The pain of losing him was indescribable. He lived with me and my everyday life was forever changed. I know the pain of loss. I also know that with each memory, every picture and endless stories, you will smile again. You will laugh, you will feel your heart start to mend. You can do this, you are not alone. You are going to be alright.

You may be stressed with money problems, kids or family life. You may feel like no one else could possibly understand what you are going through. Everyone at some point goes through this, whether they admit it or not. You need to dig deep to find your courage, you can do it. We all struggle financially, wondering how the bills will be paid, how we are going to make it this month. We all have kids that will pull us in a million different directions. You will put your needs aside for them. We all have arguments with our significant others. It is part of a relationship. Life gets hard, it gets messy, it is stressful. Believe me when I say you can do this, you are not alone. You are going to be alright.

Always remember, no matter what you are going through you are never alone. You find your courage and you will make it through. You are going to be alright.

FOR THE LOVE OF LIFE

by

Lora Ann

"Family isn't always blood. It's the people in your life who want you in theirs; the ones who accept you for who you are. The ones who would do anything to see you smile love you no matter what."

- Unknown

A high-pitched *ring* bounced off the walls across the condo, interrupting my mental checklist—plants watered, bills due next week paid, house cleaned—the persistent phone became deafening as I approached my bedroom. Reaching across the bed to answer it, "Hello," I bit out under the anxiety of making sure nothing was forgotten before I left on my trip.

"C-C-Ca-ra," came the sob on the other end, "I *need* you."

"Dee? Honey, what's wrong?" My best friend wasn't known for hysterics. Incessant pacing began on my end as every possible scenario played through my mind.

"It's Jade."

The phone fell from my hand as if something had ripped it from me. Swearing coarsely, I picked it up.

Stay calm, deep breaths, just listen. "What happened to the baby, Dee?" Fear mounted and my throat went bone dry at what I knew was coming.

"The surgery was unsuccessful. She's deteriorating at a rapid rate. Cara…if we don't find a match soon, my baby girl is going to die." Her terror-filled wails consumed me as I slid to the floor in a heap, tears streaming.

A gasp tore from me, "NO!" Jade was precious and her mom and dad wanted and prayed for her. God wouldn't just take her. Not after her valiant fight to live. There had to be a donor, a match somewhere. Anywhere. "We researched this when she was diagnosed with biliary atresia. You can use a living donor. The liver regenerates, and besides, she's what now, a twelve pound baby? She couldn't possibly need that much from anyone. I'll test for a match; we'll do what it takes."

The heavy sigh told me more than anything she could've said at that moment. My decision was made. Dee was a sister to me in all the ways that mattered. Though we didn't share DNA, we were tight. Had been since middle school when my parents decided to hit the mission field and I had no desire to go with them. They might have felt called to Africa, but I sure hadn't. I had begged and pleaded to God for my parents to stay with me as preteen, but they left anyway. Lucky for me, Dee's family offered to let me stay with them. My parents were still spreading the good news in some village in Nigeria. Could say I had abandonment issues as a result. At least, that was what my counselor had said. Then again, what the heck did he know? He only wanted to bed me at the time. "I'm coming to Salt Lake City."

Her timid, "I just didn't know who else to call," hit a spot in my heart reserved only for Dee.

"I'll be there as fast as I can."

"Wait! Don't you have trip?"

"To hell with work, Dee. You're my only family. I'm not stewing in Moscow when there's something I can do."

"And just what is that, exactly?"

"Let's see if I'm able to be her donor. Also…you need to know you're not alone and have someone there for you holding your hand through this."

We were bawling so hard we couldn't speak. I hung up with Dee and called in sick to work. No one and nothing would stop me from being there with her.

After dumping my flight bags into the closet, I grabbed a duffle bag and filled it with essentials. Once I settled into the driver's seat of my Honda Civic, the drive towards whatever the hell fate had in store for us began. *Please, God, if you're listening, don't take Jade.*

***

Ten hours of driving was plenty of time for my mind to wander to places of heartbreak. I stopped at a truck stop outside of Vegas for a much needed restroom break and more black coffee. Funny how I'd always drank coffee with cream until I became a flight attendant and began traveling overseas. Now it was straight up and strong that I preferred. Rain fell in hard blasts once I reached St. George, Utah, sounding like hundreds of insects striking the windshield and matching my tears as they stung my raw cheeks. The flash floods that were known in this area came to mind, bringing the morbid account of those who had perished in them. *Lord, I need you. Actually, Dee and Jason and Jade need you so much more.*

I pulled into Dee's driveway just after one in the morning, shocked to find her standing outside waiting for me. Too much emotion enveloped me as I slammed the car into park and jumped out while the engine was still running. As we ran towards one another, our bodies collided with enough force to rock me backwards. Sobs wracked us for quite some time before we could speak. Eventually, I turned the car off and grabbed my bag, shuffling next to her as we entered her upper middle class home.

Silence was my companion while sitting at the kitchen table as Dee busied herself with making me a snack. Always taking care of someone, it was simply her nature to nurture and why she made a phenomenal mom. Since we'd practically grown up together, I knew better than to intervene. In a way, this was therapy for her. She sat down across from me with an impressive spread for the wee hours of the morning. Small sandwiches, cheese, fruit, and a glass pitcher of lemon water—which had already been sitting there—was presented in a way that would impress Martha Stewart. Proof was in her beautiful garden out back and the small lemon tree she had planted. A watery smile crept along the corners of my mouth. "What?" she questioned.

"You're just so domestic. I'm always surprised you don't do all this in pearls and high heels."

She began to giggle, covering her mouth as she did so—the result of braces with rubber bands that had to be worn at all times during our formidable teen years. "Jason would probably enjoy that," she apprised with a wicked gleam in her eyes.

Dee met Jason our freshman year of college, falling in love hard and fast. A wedding the following summer came on the heels of her and I being hired with an airline. They had a remarkably strong marriage and had gone through so much already. Her look sobered as she slid over a folder, snapping me out of my musings. Inside I found medical consent forms. Knowledge that since Jade's surgery, known as Kasai procedure—where they used part of her intestines to build a bile duct outside her liver—had not worked, meaning the bile ducts inside her liver were the problem.

Much to our horror only a liver transplant could save her now.

My vision blurred as I skimmed over all the documentation on what was needed to be tested as Jade's living donor. Dee cleared her throat. "Jason is already about half way through the process. Cara..." her voice broke. She took a sip of water and continued, "I could only do the blood test before they ruled me out."

I gasped out, "Oh no! What's wrong?" Clasping her shaking hand, I braced myself for more bad news.

A self-deprecating smile slid along her lips. "Well, I'm—"

"Pregnant," came from across the room.

My eyes darted in that direction and lit on Jason standing in the shadows. "But Jade is only five months old," I replied dumbfounded.

"Technically we only had to wait six weeks, Cara," Jason pointed out the blatantly obvious.

With a wave of my hand I stood and declared, "Of course," turning towards the kitchen to rinse off my plate and set it in the dishwasher.

Jason chuckled deeply. "Looks as if we've embarrassed her with our scandalous activities as husband and wife."

Dee responded, "Jay, stop. She's just processing. You know she's not a prude."

His, "True that," made me blush more. He kissed Dee with enough passion I considered leaving the room as heat rose from my chest to my face. If I'd looked in a mirror, my reflection would show just how lobster-red I was. Using as much discretion as possible, I turned to busy myself by wiping down the already spotless counters. My latest romantic escapade had been with one of Jason's colleagues. God, I'd never do that again. Way too awkward when things didn't work out. And Phil had been a nice enough guy, just not the one for me. *Story of my life right there.*

Dee pulled back from Jason's attentions, playfully smacking his chest, which I caught out of my peripheral vision. "We're sorry, Cara," she apologized.

"The hell I am," Jason spoke under his breath, earning him a more forceful whack. He grumbled something incomprehensible, taking a seat at the table and digging into the goodies in front of him.

I joined them. "No need to say sorry. Not like it's anything I haven't seen before," I yawned.

Dee stood, tugging me to my feet. "Come on. Let's get you to bed. Jade will be awake before we know it."

As if the little princess had heard her mother, a loud squawk broke through the house. The precious little girl continued wailing as we entered her bedroom. "Nothing wrong with her lungs," I affirmed.

Dee laughed, picking Jade up. "There, there, little one," she whispered softly to her daughter. "Daddy is on his way with your ba-ba."

Jade was more jaundiced than I remembered. In the low light, the whites of her eyes glowed bright yellow. After Dee changed her, Jason arrived with a bottle in hand. The liquid inside looked thicker than formula. Dee had noticed my confusion. "Yes. It's a special concoction our princess here has to drink."

"An expensive brew for our lil' monster," Jason teased.

Taken back for a moment by his reference, I mentally chastised myself, *Laughter is the best medicine, and kidding around makes this grave situation a little more tolerable.* Dee placed the little princess in my arms while Jason handed me the special concoction. Softly cooing at the sweet baby in my arms, Dee and Jason gave me a hug from either side. "That probably sounded a bit cruel to you, Cara," he acknowledged, "but we've learned you have to laugh through the most difficult times to keep your sanity."

Dee stroked her daughter's head. "The alternative is just too depressing."

"You're both right. I'm tired and was just a tad surprised is all. I'm the one who should apologize."

Dee *pffed* as Jason scoffed, "Nonsense."

Dee smiled down at me. "What's with that look?"

"Just you've never been one for babies."

"Or kids in general," Jason added.

"Alright, I confess, the whole marriage and having a family makes me want to run, screaming." I glanced down at the sated Jade in my arms, drifting off to sleep. "But being an auntie to this little princess, is amazing."

Jason's hand rested on Dee's womb, the look of love and adoration shining brightly in his eyes. "Don't forget the peanut here."

"How could I?! I'll love being an auntie to all of your children."

"You can't be all about work, Cara," Jason declared. "The right man just hasn't shown up is all."

They left the room as I continued to stare down at the sleeping angel in my arms. "Mr. Right? Between you and me, Jade, I think he only exists in fairytales."

The sun peeked through the blinds, becoming an effective alarm clock. Crap, I had no intentions of falling asleep in the rocking chair while holding Jade. As I rubbed the sleep from my eyes, a blanket slid to the floor. Dee must've covered me when she came to get the baby. Stretching out the kinks in my back, I couldn't ignore how exhausted I was. Rest would have to come later on in the day. After freshening up, I went downstairs in search of everyone. Jason stood in the doorway, briefcase in hand, as he kissed Dee and Jade goodbye before leaving for work. I took Jade in my arms, giving her a gentle squeeze. "Morning, princess." Dee was already puttering around the house as I inquired, "So what are the plans for this sweet girl?"

"Well, she's already on the transplant list as a priority. In the meantime, Jason is going through a ton of medical tests like you want to do. They need to know he's in optimal health, and honestly, a related donor is more favorable. The same protocol will be in place if you're a match. Whichever one it is, Jason or you, we precede with a living transplant. A donor would keep either of you from going through the painful and dangerous surgery, not to mention long recovery."

I nodded, "Yes. But she needs a transplant soon, isn't it better if one of us can do it?"

Her hand came up swiping the tears from her cheeks. "I suppose," she swallowed hard, "I can't lose any of you."

"Oh, Dee." I walked over and wrapped an arm around her shoulders. "You cannot think like that."

She sighed, taking the fussy Jade from me. Watching mother and daughter for that tender moment made me yearn for whole line of living donors ready to help Jade. "What about other family members? Aren't they being tested, too?" When she looked down and away, I had my answer. "I see. No one else wants to go through all of that pain voluntarily." It wasn't a question. Not like I was actually looking forward to it, or that I wanted Jason to go through that either.

"In our parents' defense, they're just too old. As for the others," she added, "I've heard every excuse under the sun."

I kissed Jade's head before walking over and pulling out the forms. Without any more thought on the subject, I began filling them out.

***

Turned out, I wasn't a match for Jade. Jason had passed every medical test and the surgery was a go. As we all prepared for the inevitable, Dee and I scheduled our trips around one another so one of us was always there to care for Jade. She flew all the way up to her maternity leave, which was perfect timing.

Jade's stomach was protruding more and more each day, and her color was getting deeper and more of a ghastly yellow. She'd lost a more weight, something her fragile, ailing body just couldn't afford. The team that would perform the surgery in San Francisco decided it was time to move her and operate quickly, before she lost all hope of survival. Not news any parent wanted to hear, especially a pregnant mama.

Jason had to tie up a few more loose ends in Salt Lake before he could join us. He wanted to make sure all the i's were dotted and t's were crossed on the paperwork, since there was a chance he wouldn't pull through the surgery considering the difficult procedure. Again, we did our best not to dwell in dark places. Preferring to walk in the light and keep hope alive, each of us hanging on to faith with all we had. I felt an ominous weight pressing down and holding me prisoner. No doubt Dee and Jason could feel it, too. Beyond pissed off, I wasn't able to drop my three day trip to Frankfurt so I could drive Dee and Jade to San Francisco. "I should just call in sick," I huffed, packing.

Dee sat on the edge of the bed. "You're already in enough trouble with your absences. Fly the trip and meet us there. It's no biggie."

"Not the point, Dee. You'd think they could give me a little leeway considering the situation."

"We're not immediate family."

"The hell you aren't," I growled.

"Doesn't matter, Cara," she shrugged, "it is what it is."

Although I knew she was right, didn't mean I liked it or agreed. A far too stubborn Dee decided she would drive with Jade by herself. We argued all day over it which wasn't good for her or the baby she carried. I hoped Jason could talk some sense into her when he got home. Jason could be heard outside the house as I loaded my suitcase into the trunk. There were times, past and present, where I disagreed with Jason and the way he handled difficult situations— especially when it came to Dee. The only thing that kept me in check was his love for her and hers for him. Plus, he'd never, ever harm her physically. Past experiences with volatile men told me to proceed with caution. Jason had slowly won me over, convincing me that loud or angry didn't result in physical measures. He truly was one of the good guys, and Dee deserved a man who cherished her. By the time I left, he'd won and Dee would wait for him to drive them. *Thank you, God!*

***

Nothing could have prepared me for the transplant wing in Chilren's Hospital. Until then, I had never seen that many children in one place fighting so hard to survive. To live. Parents hoping and praying for miracles, that their children would receive transplants and pull through difficult surgeries in order to have a chance at life. I'd never truly grasped the magnitude of what Dee and Jason and

Jade were facing. There was no time for me to process as Dee stepped out of the room, hand over her mouth, as she fought to contain herself. Her body was in the throes of deep shudders, reminding me of the jolt experienced during an earthquake, and clued me in that she wasn't getting sick, she was sobbing.

I rushed to meet her at the door, wrapping my arms tightly around her. She clutched my shirt tightly and let all of that pent up fear pour out with each tear and gasp. At that moment, I had no words to say. Quite frankly they seemed hollow to me, somehow false. There was nothing I could offer she hadn't heard before. As if I spoke any platitude, she'd be harmed in some way. Though, I fully understood that it was how many dealt with difficult, unbearable circumstances. Not wrong, just wasn't me. A hug or holding someone's hand could say a thousand words. Dee needed to know she wasn't alone. After several long minutes, Dee choked out, "Sh-She's getting w-w-worse, Cara. My ba-by is so sick." The last word ripped from her soul.

Due to health issues, her parents were unable to be there. "Can you walk?" She nodded. I held her hand snuggly as we made our way out to the garden, sitting in her favorite spot by the roses. "Are they prepping Jason?"

"No. He had to step away for a few minutes."

"Is his mom still coming?"

"She's flying out here tomorrow." She gasped out, "Oh God, I have to tell her they've moved the surgery."

"She'll be okay, Dee. Please don't worry."

Jason's mother had planned to be here to care for her son. All of that had been prearranged. Honestly, what could I possibly say to make this easier? She could lose both her husband and daughter in surgery. Jason was dealing with the real possibility of losing his child, or sending his wife into a nervous breakdown. Worse, due to stress, Dee could lose the child she was carrying. Neither one of them was in a good place at the moment. Both needed someone to lean on. Whether I felt equipped to do so, the fact remained; I was the one present and accounted for. Or as my mother would say, *"You were called for such a time as this."* How I wished my mother was there. She'd have all the right words and beautiful prayers to offer.

A nurse met us with a wild look in her eyes. Immediately, we jumped to our feet from the bench we'd been sitting on. "Is something wrong?" I inquired with deep trepidation.

"Could be something very good," she replied cautiously. "Follow me, please."

Hand in hand we trailed behind the nurse, arriving in Jade's room where Jason and the whole team were waiting. Jason walked over to his wife and held her tightly as he whispered over her head, "Thank you," to me.

I inclined my head as the lead surgeon began to explain what was happening. Seemed a donor was on the way via helicopter as he spoke. They were taking Jade back and prepping her in the event the liver was sustainable. "If the donor liver isn't viable, we'll go ahead and operate on Jason," the doctor clarified.

Jason blanched into a spooky shade of white with that information. Further reason was given, "Jade is out of time." The lead surgeon expounded, "If we wait any longer, the surgery will be impossible."

We all knew what that meant: Jade will die.

Dee and Jason held each other and sobbed. It was such a private moment that I stepped out with the team. They left in a hurry, practically jogging down the hall to do their job. A few, I noticed, stayed behind. The door opened and Jason was in a wheelchair. He stopped the nurse who was pushing him by putting his hand up. "Just a minute, please." Locking his gaze on mine, he offered that same hand. I grasped him tightly as he spoke, "Promise me...you'll stay with Dee. She can't be left alone, Cara."

I leaned down and kissed his wet cheek. "Always. You can count on me. I'll be here every step of the way."

"You are priceless," he swallowed hard, "and we are so grateful to have you in our lives. There's no way we could have gotten through this without you."

I nodded and managed to add, "I'm so glad we're friends, Jason."

"Back attcha."

We hugged before he was taken to be prepped for surgery. I wouldn't permit my thoughts to go to sad places. Jason would be fine. Jade would get through this. The thundering of a helicopter brought Dee to my side in the hallway. She clutched my hand and hurried out to the balcony area off the waiting room. The whirlybird hovered above the landing pad as we watched, holding our ears from the deafening sound. Without warning, Dee began to scream at the top of her lungs, "THIS ISN'T FAIR! How could *you* do this?!" She pointed at the dark sky before completely losing all sense of composure and beat the railing with her fists.

Dread filled me and gripped my gut like a vice. What if she hurt herself? Could she harm the baby in her womb? I clutched her shoulders and pulled her against my body, encircling her arms so she'd stop hitting things. We slid to cold, hard cement. She kept repeating, "What kind of monster am I?" over and over.

I yanked her head back so she had to look sideways and back at me. "You are *not* a monster! Do you hear me?"

"I am, Cara," she replied quietly. "Yes, I am,"

Confusion knit my brow, self-blame could not enter this situation. "How do you figure?"

"I'm actually happy that someone else has just lost their child. If that doesn't make me something *vile*, then what does?"

Damn! I was in no way prepared for that answer. "Being happy that your precious little girl has a donor doesn't make you a horrible person."

She shook her head and stood. "I'm not asking you to agree with me, Cara." She walked back inside as I fought my own emotions. *God, if you really did call me for this, then you need to help me out here. I'm not strong enough.*

***

We sat in silence waiting for some word, any news at all, about what was happening with Jason, Jade, and the donor. What felt like hours had actually been about sixty minutes when one of the doctors from the team stepped out to talk to us. "The donor's liver was damaged beyond use."

There was no controlling the tears sliding down my face. Dee had been right about one thing, another mommy had just lost her precious child. Things really could be unfair, far beyond our understanding. Dee was allowed back to see Jason before they went ahead with his surgery. I slid to my knees in the waiting room and prayed fervently.

Word finally came that Jason's surgery had been a success. He was in recovery as they took Jade in. Dee turned to me and I asked, "Will you go to the chapel with me?"

After all these years, my best friend wanted to step into a church. What that meant exactly I didn't know, but something told me it was significant. Once more, I sat quietly holding Dee, my sister, as she faced the most difficult trial of her life. Many would never go through such an experience in their lifetime. Then again, many would face worse. Somewhere in there she broke the silence with, "You know I was actually blaming myself for this." I tried to say something to refute that, but she stopped me with her hand over my mouth. "Please. Let me confess." I nodded, squeezing her hand. "At first, I thought, wow, I must have really been an awful person to deserve this. Then I thought of every single wrongdoing I had ever done, totally agreeing, yeah, I did deserve it. But you," she turned her body so we were knee to knee, "you made me recognize that's not how things work. He doesn't operate that way. And as that truth filled me, I came to realize that my little girl has a purpose. What it is, I don't know yet. But there is a reason."

I shook my head, wiping away the tears. "All I've done is be here for you."

She grabbed a hold of my face. "Don't you see just what that means? You've been here every step of the way. That's love, Cara."

What could I say? Love was more than a feeling, it was action.

Eventually, we went to see Jason. He looked so pale and weak. Yet the smile that lit up his eyes when Dee walked into the room was beautiful. Priceless. Love was shining through in all its brilliant glory. We received word Jade was out of surgery and doing remarkably well. Dee and I went to be with her. Though I hated seeing that sweet princess hooked up to so many machines, I was also past grateful for such technology.

Loved ones came and went throughout the week. Jason was regaining his strength and even made it down via wheelchair to see his little girl. Jade continued to grow stronger and stronger. We all knew she would have set backs, and that she could be on immunosuppression medication to keep her body from rejecting her new liver. Jason's would fully regenerate. Truly a miracle had taken place right before my eyes. How that would affect the rest of my life, only time would tell. However, four lives were altered beyond measure an experience none of us would be able to keep quiet about. It was a story of love, friendship, and sacrifice—one of unfailing hope. Mom was right, sometimes what appears to be the worst thing life could give you, turned into the most amazing. After all, there was a reason so many referred to it as beauty painted with ashes.

***

Christmas held more wonder that year than any other. Jason was released a couple of weeks post-surgery, but it was a slow healing process. Jade spent a month in the hospital recuperating. She'd always carry the physical scar of her ordeal as would Jason with his upside down T scar on his abdomen, which staff at the hospital called his "Mercedes" mark. The bond that had formed between father and daughter was enough to steal one's breath away. Dee and the baby growing inside her were doing absolutely spectacular. The little bundle of joy was due to arrive in February.

I sat taking in the happy scene before me. Dee handed me the last present under the tree. "This is from Jade," she explained, kissing the sleeping princess.

I stroked Jade's downy cheek. "Thank you." I opened my gift and gasped. "Oh!" Nestled inside was a frame. On one side was her handprints in plaster, the other side held a candid picture of me holding her in ICU. I remembered that night. She'd been restless, and I'd been given permission to hold her. We rocked in the chair as I sang a Welsh lullaby "All Through The Night" to soothe her.

Underneath the picture was engraved:

To the bes auntie a girl could ever be blessed with.
Thank you for being there for me and loving me.
All my love, Jade Yvonne Stromer.

Tears fell onto my hands as I took the little princess into my arms and whispered, "I'd do it all again for you." Softly I kissed her cheek. "I love you so." Truly I was the one who'd been blessed. For one never knew when they would be called upon to assist an angel.

SECOND CHANCES

by

Airicka Phoenix

Jacob wasn't a believer of things unanswerable. All things had answers; all things had a scientific explanation. But Angie had none of those things.

He could find no method to her madness, no sense to her constant ability to see things in Technicolor when life was a murky shade of gray. How could one person be so… carefree? Normal people weren't so happy!

It was unnatural.

"Stop frowning, Jake." Her fingers were warm, prodding the corners of his mouth. Her laugh tinkled when he jerked back. "You're going to get wrinkles."

"I'm seventeen," he rubbed the tingling spot on his face. "I won't get wrinkles for another twenty years."

Again, she laughed, leaping to her feet and doing a twirl right there on the winding path cutting through the park. Her hair splayed out in the air, a glistening cape of shiny copper.

"Come on, Jake! Let's go do something fun!"

Fun? For him, that would be going home and looking over his biology paper. But with her, it could mean anything.

"Like what?"

Angie shrugged her dainty shoulder. "Let's go to the cliffs. It's almost sunset."

"There's a sixty percent chance it's going to rain—"

She rolled her pretty green eyes heavenwards, an endearing smile tilting her lips. "You are always so serious! Besides, I think it would be romantic to be caught in the rain together."

Jacob couldn't help wrinkle his nose. "What's so romantic about pneumonia?"

She shook her head, swooping down and grabbing his wrist. "Come on, Mr. Stick-In-The-Mud."

As affronted as he was by the name-calling, he allowed himself to be yanked out of his seat and dragged to the other end of the park.

The cliffs overlooked a wide stretch of ocean, now churning with an impending storm. The sky in the distance was a murky gray, bleeding into the red and orange. In his opinion, there was nothing remotely romantic about standing there with nothing but a painful death looming below them. However, Angie seemed pleased; she had a flush to her cheeks and a glow to her eyes that made them appear glassy. He would have been concerned if it wasn't an expression she wore often whenever they were together.

"Jake?" she turned those enormous eyes towards him. "Do you ever wish you could fly?"

Jacob thought about it as carefully as he would any other question before answering, "Well, that depends on what you mean. Do I think I'll sprout wings and take to the heavens? Then no, I don't."

There was a strange darkness in her eyes when she looked away, a flicker Jacob had never seen before. It was unlike her not to be glowing from the inside out.

"I always wish I could fly. I would go everywhere."

He started to tell her it was theoretically impossible; the world was too big for a single person to see everywhere in one lifetime. But something in the way she sighed kept him in check.

Then, just like that, she was smiling again, big and bright, eyes a little wild. "Hey, you know what we should do? We should jump!"

Maybe it was the glint behind her stare or the way her grip on his hand had tightened, but Jacob shuffled back a step. "What?"

"Come on! It'll be so much fun!"

"No!" He shook her hand off. "There are rocks at the bottom. The probability of us missing them—"

There was no smile on her face this time when she rolled her eyes. "Don't be such a baby! We'll aim away from the rocks."

"The winds are too strong!" Was he really standing there arguing this with her? "We're not jumping!"

"I am!" Then she was running, like a gazelle through the meadows.

For a moment, all he saw was floating hair, the billow of her skirt fluttering around her long legs. Her laughter caught the whistling wind and pounded in his ears. His heart jacked into his throat, stopping possibly all together if he could wrap his head around it. Every nerve in his body screamed as image-after-image flashed behind his eyes of her sailing over and disappearing from sight, from his life forever.

"No!" The scream tore his esophagus.

He couldn't recall lunging after her. He wasn't even sure when he'd moved. But he had her, a fistful of her dress in his grasp. Her yelp of surprise had never sounded so beautiful to him. He reeled her in like a fish on a hook, yanking her into the folds of his arms, crushing her.

"Are you crazy!" he growled into the top of her head. "Don't ever do that again!"

"I won't." There was a hint of a smile in her tone, but he didn't care when her arms found their way around him too.

SOMEONE TO TURN TO

by

Ella Medler

"In the depth of winter, I finally learned that within me there lay an invincible summer."

- Albert Camus

This story is dedicated to all those who need a reason to look for strength inside their own soul.

The smoke was choking me, so I knew Emi was feeling it too. Just then, he sneezed and spluttered into my t-shirt, leaving behind a glistening trail of snot that stretched between my torso and his nose. Gross. A sickly looking moon spared the world just enough light for me to see the mess and curse the need to look after him. My little brother — the bane of my existence.

He sniffled and nuzzled his little face against me, spreading the snot widely across my front. Without thinking, I put my arm around his shoulders and hugged him tighter. For a fleeting moment, I questioned the incomprehensible pathways of my brain — logically, I should have pushed him away — but there was no time to dwell on the whys and maybes. This was a scary situation and we had to come out of it alive, somehow. Keeping Emi quiet was crucial to us remaining undetected, and therefore safe.

Worry about my mother clouded my thoughts and suddenly I felt weak and useless. Her eyes had been fierce with worry as she smashed the lock off the old dryer's door and helped us inside. Then her footsteps disappeared in the direction of the front yard. Even from here, stuck as we were inside a metal box lost among so many other lumps of scrap, trash and useless junk that filled the garden, I'd heard her voice once or twice, so I knew she was alive.

There were other noises, cracking and snapping in the night, and the smoke was sure indication that something was on fire — the house, probably, or maybe the car. Not knowing what was going on was killing me, but Mama's last words to me had been, "Look after Emilio. Keep him safe." So I did.

It was the hardest thing I'd done in my life, I was sure. Even harder than telling the police that Papa was dangling from the willow, two years prior. The only thing that stopped me from bursting out of our make-shift safety pod right now was the fact that I could hear her voice.

Hers and those of the worthless degenerates who had come chasing after us yet again.

We'd probably have to leave this place and move once more. I was used to it. It wouldn't be the first time we'd had to run away, and my guess was that this wouldn't be the last time, either.

But it was the first time I had caused it.

***

Up until four weeks ago life was tough. We never seemed to have enough of anything, after Papa passed away — food or clothes or shoes… But we were happy together and we made the best of each day. We went to school, played in the stream on hot days, and cuddled up with Mama under the threadbare blanket on the saggy-bottomed couch when the nights were chilly. We understood each other. Sometimes, we wouldn't even need to speak to know what the others were thinking. We made a perfect little team of three.

Then Mama let her guard down and a man in. He brought trouble. Not a bad man, Rudy — though he could never be as good as my papa — but his needs were simple and his manner straight. You knew when he was in a good mood and when it would be best to disappear. He drank, but not enough to be abusive. He was okay.

Rudy spent a lot of time with Mama, which meant I had Emi hanging from my coat most of the time, but I didn't begrudge her the little happiness she felt. I just took Emi out of the house to give them some privacy.

Until, one night, a strange car stopped outside and a pair of rough-looking men the size of small houses dragged him out of the back seat and up the porch steps. Rudy was slurring his words and soon collapsed face-down on the couch. Mama pushed us into the bedroom and the look in her eyes warned me not to argue. She mouthed at me to lock the door, so I did what she asked and locked

Emi in the closet, too, as a precaution. I opened the window a crack, for a quick getaway, then went and stuck my ear to the door to hear what was going on.

I caught only too clearly the pleas of my mother as she tried in vain to revive Rudy. All the while, the strange men shouted about payment she owed their boss and how no matter how far she'd run, they would track her down and make her pay. Her and her kids.

Things were smashing on the floor, and Mama screamed. That was when I slipped through the window and went back in through the front door.

One of the men had Mama by the hair and the other was pushing her to her knees. I stood rooted to the spot, terrified. Then I must have made a sound; three pairs of eyes locked on me.

"Run!" Mama shrieked, at the same time as the one holding her hair shouted "Get her!"

I ran. I ran like I'd never run before. I vaulted over the piles of trash in the back yard, tripped through the thicket, dodged the trees at top speed all the way through the woods and tiptoed across the fallen tree trunk until I was across the water and into the wilder forest to the north. For hours, I crouched behind a bush and waited for my doom. It didn't come.

When I was brave enough to return, I approached the house cautiously. The strange car was gone, and Mama was in the kitchen, laboring over the sink. She saw me and waved me in, wiped her tears from her eyes, then sent me to bed, assuring me she would follow shortly when she saw I didn't want to leave her side. She hugged us tight that night, all night long, and we slept on top of each other in the double bed while Rudy slept off his drink on the couch.

That was the first time we had trouble, and I knew there were many other times when those men had returned, but Mama somehow managed to keep them and us apart. Rudy left after a while, never to come back, but as I'd never needed anyone other than Mama and Emi in my life, I didn't miss him.

It was February now, and Emi had just turned seven. Soon it would be my fifteenth birthday. I was dreaming of a nice dress I could perhaps wear for Prom, but if that wasn't possible, then I would be happy to spend a couple of hours at the Arcade, watching my friends play. It would be almost as good as playing myself. Probably better. I didn't know how to play those games anyway, so I would probably waste my quarters if I had any.

Mama's scream pulled me out of my contemplation, and the shrill sound of pain in her voice pierced my heart with worry. I wanted to run over to her, but Emi's hands were clutched around my neck. She screamed again and he tightened his grip. I rubbed my hand in circles on his back to calm him, but shoved the drier door open with my toes anyway, my decision taken.

***

I didn't know whether it would be safe to get out, but Emi had promised to stay put until I came back for him. In return, I had to promise that I wouldn't leave him. Ugh. I didn't want to leave him, and at the same time I did. There was so much I couldn't do with Emi stuck to my side like a limpet. He didn't make friends easily, and hadn't yet developed the thick skin he'd need to survive a life of hardship. So he ended up alone and in tears more often than not. He didn't have anyone else to turn to, other than Mama and me.

The heat and smoke brought tears to my eyes as soon as I peeked out of my shelter. Tongues of flame curled around the first floor of our house, the heat coiling around my body unpleasantly, even at this distance. Mama was nowhere to be seen.

I stole around like a shadow, from pile of trash to broken appliance to another heap of junk, keeping my distance from the fire, until I got close enough to see around the side of the house.

I spotted Mama at the same time I heard the blaring of the fire engine way off, closer to town. She was leaning against the side of a dirty white van with the side door open. Three men stood between us, doing something I couldn't quite see. One grabbed her face roughly in his hand and leaned over her. He shouted something, but she didn't look scared or worried by his words.

"I told you, you have that wrong," she said as I made myself one with the mud and slithered closer, the darkness and thick smoke covering the ground now my new best allies.

"We've gotta go before the fire crew arrives," one of the others said and got into the driver's seat.

"Fine." Mama shrugged and put one foot in the van. The man who was leaning over her stopped her. She turned to him. "I said I will come willingly. What else can I do?"

"Get your children—"

"How many times… Are you deaf? They ran away weeks ago, the first time you came over — and good riddance. I couldn't wait to be rid of them… couldn't afford to feed them anyway."

"You stupid bitch!" The guy's fist connected with the side of her head and she collapsed inside the vehicle. "We could have used them."

She spat and drew back, pulling herself into a ball on the floor of the van.

I wanted to run to her and rescue her, but something held me rooted to the spot, wondering whether she really wanted to be rescued. Her next words ripped a hole straight through my heart, stopping dead any wish I may have had to help her.

"The kids were a waste of space. I didn't want them, and you wouldn't have wanted them either. They're gone — dead, for all I know. I have no children. Besides," she smiled an ugly smile I'd never seen on her face before, "Life's gonna be much more fun without them."

I gasped loud enough to hear it distinctly against the noise of the fire. The roaring of it as it tore through the house doubled in volume all of a sudden, or maybe it was just the rush of blood through my temples, the tearing of my heart.

She didn't want us. No one would. Life wasn't fun with us around.

No, life wasn't fun. She was right about that… But all our smiles and jokes and cuddles? The memories we'd made together? They were all lies? I couldn't believe that.

Threads of thoughts were snarling up into knots as I struggled to make sense of her meaning. *A waste of space… I have no children.*

A nagging voice at the back of my mind was telling me she was only protecting us, somehow, as if we could ever survive without her. *I said I will come willingly. Willingly…* She was really leaving us behind; there was no other way to take that.

"Come on. Let's go. I've wasted enough of my life in this dump."

It was her voice, speaking those words, making my blood turn cold under my hot skin, already scorched red-raw and sore by the fire. She really wanted to get away. The van's door sliding shut brought the finality of her decision to my mind, and the fight back to my senses.

I have no children. I didn't want them. A waste of space.

The phrases repeated in my mind as I shot to my feet and watched the vehicle containing half of my life, my only buoy in the storms of this existence, disappear.

I have no children… Life's gonna be more fun without them.

She may have given me up heartlessly, but I was not going to drown. Not me. Not ever.

***

The fire engine rounded the corner into our muddy lane. Its bright lights blinded me, and in my hurry to get away, I fell back into a patch of nettles. Their sting was nothing compared to the agony in my heart. Still, I had made my decision, and while I'd hurt for now, I knew I wouldn't for much longer.

I staggered back through the ruined remnants of my home — my life — to the broken dryer. Emi took one look at me and began to cry. I pulled him out and dragged him into the woods. He was infuriatingly slow, and clumsier than usual. I could swear he tripped on every root, tangled into every brush, fell over every pebble. Eventually, he pulled his hand out of mine, and I let him go. I didn't even look back as I hurried forward, across the creek and away from it all.

"Wait, Carrie," his thin voice came through the night. "Wait for me!" Again, more shrill this time, more fearful. "Carrie! Carrie, you promised. You promised not to leave me. Please, Carrie, please…" And his voice dissolved into heartbreaking sobs. So I stopped and waited.

Today, I would let him have me. Tomorrow, I would be free.

***

If you follow the woods on the narrow path for a few minutes, then turn west at the thorny thicket that surrounds the patch of old birch trees, you eventually get to Old Mae's rotten yard and her vegetable garden. It's a good two-hour walk if you stay focused and don't waste time gawking after wildlife, but it looks like it will take me twice as long with Emi in tow.

I'd never taken him with me before, and I really hated to have to do it now. Old Mae's vegetable garden was a good fallback for when I was really hungry, and I'd raided it many times before, but I'd been careful to only take what I needed and no more. I didn't want to attract attention and lose one of my best foraging places.

No one knew Mae, and I'd never seen her with visitors. I was sure not even Mama knew about her. Mae lived alone, and while her place was a dump, she had many outbuildings. That was a good thing; I was planning to use one of these for a stop tonight, and then move on without Emi. It was the right time to make a clean break — hadn't I always wished that I could ditch my brother? Well, now I was getting my wish.

She'd get a mighty surprise, Old Mae, when she found Emi sleeping in a shed, or maybe when she'd catch him munching on her roots or drinking her water, but they could help each other, or if the worst came to the worst maybe she would put him in care. Whichever way, I had enough to worry about without worrying about Emi and Mae, too.

Ages later, deep into the night, I found what I'd been looking for. With little trouble, I managed to wrench open the door to some shed that seemed to house everything, from muddy old boots to bags of fertilizer, tangled twine, rubber hoses, tools and an old sawhorse surrounded by mounds of sawdust she'd obviously never cleaned away. I was certain she'd not been in here in weeks, or months, or maybe even years. Emi was dead on his feet, so I made him a little nest out of sawdust and bags; he curled up in there and was asleep before I could get to the door.

I sat in the doorway and waited for dawn, all the while planning where to go next and what to do. I would aim for a big city and see if I could find work. There had to be something I could do to pay for some food and shelter. I didn't need much, I already knew that. And school was out. There would be no time for study while I was busy staying alive. Maybe later, when I was settled, I could finish my secondary education.

Since Papa's struggle with depression I'd had this dream of being able to figure out a way to help people like him, make them happy again. I'd tried and tried, but nothing worked for Papa.

Probably because all those people who'd written the advice in the books hadn't had to actually live with his kind of demons.

But I'd known him and his demons well, I'd lived in their shadow long enough, and I still harbored a huge amount of guilt — at not being able to help him, not finding the right treatment, not being more aware, or closer, or not staying at home that day when he'd decided he'd finally had enough. Maybe if I'd spent more time in the library, looking for answers, or if I'd gone and asked the librarian for help, or something — anything — maybe that might have kept him alive.

And maybe, if Papa had stayed alive, maybe then Mama wouldn't have left me and Emi behind, to have a *fun life without us*.

Somehow, I felt I'd caused all this mayhem. I should have been able to find a cure for Papa, a better gift for Mama's birthday, stayed hidden when those thugs were attacking her, so maybe they would not have had a reason to come back… Maybe if I'd have been able to teach Emi how to deal with life better, how to be more help to her and to himself, maybe then she wouldn't have left. But I was kidding myself. She'd never wanted us, we were a waste of space, so she'd moved on, to a better life.

Well, I was determined to move on, too.

I turned to look at Emi, sleeping peacefully in his makeshift bed, and tried to imagine how much happier he would be without me. He'd forget me in a few weeks, for sure. Then he could have a happier life, like Mama would, and me too.

Unbidden, memories of smiles and shrieks of laughter, and Mama's last birthday came into my mind. We'd decorated the house with bunting made of paper napkins I'd stolen from a town fair one weekend, and I wrote *Happy Birthday* on the tiny triangles for the occasion. I'd even managed to scrounge enough money together to get her a little present — a charm bracelet, with only one charm on it: a little heart-shaped padlock with a tiny key. I'd paid for it all with real cash, so no one could come back later and accuse her of having stolen it.

My gift was so much better than Emilio's. He'd given her an empty cereal box which he said was full of kisses. She's smiled and hugged him like she had me, but what kind of birthday present was that?

No wonder she'd left us. We really weren't enough to make her happy. The sooner I accepted that, the sooner I could get on with my life, and Emilio with his.

I decided that as soon as it was light enough I'd get some fruit or roots from the garden and set them by his side, and then I'd go. No need for teary goodbyes, no need for any more heartbreak. I would stop dwelling on Mama's words before nightfall. As for Emi... he'd find a way to cope.

***

The sun blinded me when I opened my eyes. Immediately, a shadow slid in front of me, cutting the glare and giving me a chance to open my eyes fully.

"Come inside if you want a hot drink."

Old Mae turned around and started making her way toward the house without waiting for an answer. Emi shot to his feet and leaned on my shoulder, looking after her. Then he strode past me and took a couple of steps after Mae. He seemed to remember something, all of a sudden. His eyes were huge and tearful when he turned, and he launched himself at me from that distance. I caught him and held him tight, letting him sob into my t-shirt again, all the while cursing the fact that I'd been weak enough to fall asleep when I should have walked away.

By the time he'd settled into quiet sobs I decided I could stay one more day. I took his hand and led them to Old Mae's kitchen.

The difficulty arose when the old woman tried talking to him, and Emi didn't utter a sound. I couldn't understand how such a noisy little boy could turn into a mute overnight. Mae didn't think it odd at all. "It's the shock," she explained, then bustled to the pantry, reappearing with a jar of preserved fruit in her hand.

She dished out breakfast — toast topped with this gooey, sweet fruit preserve, and mugs of hot milk for all of us — and asked me to tell her what had happened. I did so in few words, leaving out the nasty details, because I really didn't want to make it worse for Emi. When he'd finished his toast, Mae gave him a dented metal bowl and sent him to the garden to look for any berries he could find. He wouldn't find any — it was February. But I welcomed the chance to speak without fear.

So I told Mae all that I'd heard Mama say, and how I felt about it.

"What are your intentions with Emi?" she asked.

I didn't answer. She could see it in my eyes. Prickly silence stretched between us for a while, but I didn't break it.

"If I chuck you out, you'll dump him somewhere else." It wasn't a question. I didn't feel it required an answer.

"What about your school?" I shrugged. "I thought you wanted to do something with your life. At least that's what the librarian told me."

She had my attention with that one statement. How come she and the librarian had talked? About me, no less? I'd thought Mae never went anywhere or met anyone.

Mae humphed at the questions in my eyes.

"I'll make a deal with you," she said. "You stay here with him, and I'll sign any paperwork the school sends home as if I were your mom. I'll give you a roof and food, and in exchange you finish your schooling, young lady. Any trouble and you're both out."

I said I'd give it a try, for a week maybe, or until summer, though I wasn't convinced this unlikely arrangement would ever work. Before long, I realized my expectations had been wrong. I didn't really care for Mae, but it was hard to walk away from Emi. As much as he annoyed me, I found he needed me… or maybe I needed him. He never spoke of the night when our mother left, and I didn't bring it up.

Mae proved to be a good host, though we never felt the warmth or fell into the crazy laughter we had when Mama was around. She kept her end of the bargain, so I did mine. Emi took it harder than I thought, losing Mama, and whether involuntarily or through his own will, he never spoke aloud again. In fact, his last words had been his plea for me not to leave him, that night, as we ran through the forest. I often wondered, in the years that followed, whether he saw it as a secret pact between us — as long as he kept quiet, I wouldn't leave him behind. His sudden muteness meant Mae had to find him special schooling, which he attended one day a week, alongside his usual classes. He became quite independent, and that made me proud — and free.

***

At the beginning of my senior year, Mae sat me down and we went through my options. My grades had been good, so I had a chance to follow my dream, if I so wished. I did. Nothing would have made me happier than to be able to do something worthwhile with my life, and I realized that, subconsciously, I had favored courses that would line up with the guilt I felt for not being able to help Papa. Psychology it was, then. I wouldn't fight it, but rather use it to fuel my passion.

Mae helped me fill in the forms, and where she couldn't, the librarian — who was a good friend of hers — did. Between us, I felt we did all that was in our power to ensure I could go to college, except being able to afford any fees. For that, we would look at some scholarships, and I would be looking for jobs close to campus. I'd never been afraid to work, and I was comfortable enough by now with the knowledge that Emi would be in good hands. My life was looking up.

I should have known better. Christmas brought a wave of damp cold that affected Mae's lungs more than ours. We were all hacking and wheezing, but there came a day when I knew she needed to see a doctor. Her friend, the librarian, came by to pick her up in her nice car, and we heard no more for nine whole days. I kept the house running as I always did, and made sure Emi attended school when the term restarted.

Then, one late evening, the librarian's car appeared at Mae's door. I rushed to peek into the back, but there was no one there. The biggest weight in the world dropped into my stomach as I took in the librarian's solemn expression.

Mae was gone. Her age and weakened body couldn't fight pneumonia.

We were alone again.

Hours, days and weeks passed by and I don't remember much of that time at all. I kept feeding Emi and making sure he went to school, and I went too, mostly because it gave me the illusion of a normal life. The librarian kept crossing paths with me, and though she smiled at me every time, I couldn't return the gesture.

Then one day she didn't smile, but instead drew me to a side and told me that Mae's long-lost son had been located and he would come to the house shortly, to assess its value. He wanted to sell it.

Mae had a son? It was bewildering to me that I didn't even know that. I nodded, mumbled something about being late for class and hustled away, numb and cold, unable to take in all the implications of what looked to be yet another obstacle in my way. Life could be so cruel.

That night, instead of sleeping, I stayed up and thought.

I thought about Mae and her way of life — so simple, and yet so pleasant. I thought about her kindness and generosity, and considered how easy it would have been to turn us both away. Instead, she'd fed and housed us for three years, even after death. It was three years almost to the day, when Mama… when we came over and huddled in Mae's shed.

I wouldn't think of Mama, not when there were people who had cared more about us, did more for us, people who didn't think we were a waste of space. People like Mae, who had believed in us, in our abilities to make something of our lives — even us, Carrie and Emi, the homeless orphans on the edge of complete destitution.

Mae, who helped me apply for scholarships, Mae, who always cheered for us when we did well, Mae, who kept on living… I stifled a sob, though I couldn't stop the silent tears. After a while, I wiped them all off my face. It was time to decide what to do. One thing was for sure: I hadn't fought so hard to get my dream only to have it yanked out of my reach with a few short months to go.

***

So here I was, six months later, in the antechamber of the man who could make or break my life, and Emi's with it. This man in front of me, smoking his cigar, was the benefactor who could assign me the scholarship that would put me through the course I needed. In my hand, I held tightly the many-times folded piece of paper that Mae had shown me all those months ago, with all the requirements for this scholarship listed in a neat column. I felt I had surpassed them all.

For six months I'd flitted between Mae's house and the ruin of our old burnt-out one, making sure we were never found. Once or twice, we'd had to camp out in the forest, but Emi didn't once complain, nor had he said a word in all that time. He was quite good at improvising shelters and making a good fire by now. Our team had shrunk, but we still worked well together.

I'd toiled in Mae's garden at night, when Emi was asleep, and I'd gone to school in the day. I'd applied for guardianship of my brother and got it, with the help of the librarian. When it became clear we needed a constant stream of income, I'd done my classmates' homework for them, babysat, cared for their pets, and a million other little jobs.

The short of it was that I knew I could make my life happen now. I knew that I was a survivor, and hopefully I had been able to show Emi that he was one, too.

Yes, that was a better way to look at it.

The man behind that door had the power to make life hard for me, but he couldn't break me. Whatever his decision would be, I would follow my dream.

Little did I know, by the end of the day my dream had grown exponentially, and my decisions were about to make my life both bliss and torture, heaven and hell, ecstasy and misery, and all because of one young man: Blaze Ackerman. Blaze Ackerman, the lion-hearted, my life, my punishment, my soul.

***

This exclusive story forms the background of a new uplifting series of books, the Lionheart Series, which follows the journey of two people through the challenges posed by life with PTSD. Carrie sees it from the outside, Blaze from within. If you'd like to know their stories, look for them on Amazon. Searching for Ella Medler will take you to the right place.

THE GOLDEN PAVILION

by

Bernard Tristan Foong

"When you are in harmony with yourself everything unfolds with grace and ease."

- Panache Desai

This story is dedicated to teachers, educators, and tutors who had groomed and provided sound advice to students the world over.

"I was lucky that I met the right mentors and teachers at the right moment who taught me to believe in myself."

1967
In Kinkaku-ji

This Zen Buddhist temple, the Temple of the Golden Pavilion, was located in the heart of Kyoto. It is an excellent example of Muromachi design; a minimalistic approach, recreating a larger landscape around a single opulent gold-leafed structure. Kinkaku-ji (the Temple of the Golden Pavilion) or Rokuon-ji (Deer Garden Temple) is an ancient Japanese architectural wonder. However, the present pavilion dates only from 1955: it was rebuilt after a schizophrenic monk, Hayashi Yoken, burned the original structure down. Yoken's story and Kinkaku-ji was made famous in 1958 by the renowned 20th century Japanese author and revolutionary, Mishima, who was nominated for the literary Nobel Prize three times during his life. Mishima's death was as dramatic as the temple's arson – he and his private militia took over a government building, where he gave a speech on a balcony before proceeding indoors to commit *Seppuku,* a Japanese form of ritualistic suicide by disembowelment.

It was at this tranquil Deer Garden Temple that our final segment of *Sacred Sex in Sacred Places* was filmed. As was our photographers' ritual, our entourage assembled at the Kinkaku-ji in the wee hours of dawn, before the tourists arrived en mass to view this ancient monument.

At the first glow of an autumnal morning, when the rising sun was just peeping its golden head over the horizon, Andy and Keiko were called to position by our photographers. When it came time for my Valet to simulate a love-making scene with Keiko, their rapport was one of true lovers rather than models or actors playing an intimate scene. Andy's enthusiasm and the Eurasian's avidity sparked an ineffable jealousy within me. An overwhelming invidiousness washed over my person. I hated myself for this negativity, yet my covetousness also inflamed a sexual curiosity I had never felt before. I watched the two paramours with incongruous intensity as the tantalizing eroticism was enacted. Like Mario and Aziz's camera lenses, I, too, was enthralled by their vehemence. Their arousing prelude seemed to defy rationality. They glided with serenity and grace like a pair of flittering dragonflies who were to merge into an inseparable pulsating organism. Magnetized by their intrinsic quiddity, I envisaged Andy's and my love-making. Insurmountable questions whirled in my swirling mind:

- Was this the same kind of alluring magnificence that captivated our *Sacred Sex in Sacred Places* photographers when Andy and I made love?
- Is this that certain chemistry that transforms the mundane into magic when the lovers are unperturbed, relaxed and self-possessed?
- Is this the 'look of love' that Shakespearean sonnets and Byronic heroes so wordily described throughout the ages?
- Am I witnessing the love between my Valet and me being played out by Andy and Keiko?

Thrown off by my preoccupation, I did not detect the sheik standing next to me. He whispered in my ear, *"This is art in motion. It is like watching you and your chaperone copulate."* He continued as he directed his gaze towards the copulating couple, *"Sex is indeed wholly satisfying when 2 affectionate people emerge unanxious, rewarded, and ready for more."*

I was caught off guard and did not know how to respond to his observations. Seeing my cheerlessness, he inquired, *"Do I detect traces of jealousy in your spirit, my boy?"*

"I'm not the jealous type," I lied.

"Ahh Hah! I don't believe you. I think you are not being truthful," the Arab declared.

I turned away sheepishly.

"Don't forget I'm a doctor; I've taken psychiatric seminars to know when a person is not jocund. I can tell when my patient is unhappy.

"Tell me what's bothering you, young man," he pressed.

Subduing Jealousy

Finally, I turned to face my friend, my eyes about to burst into tears. Fahrib took my hand and guided me to the terrace overlooking onto the glistening lake and tranquil gardens. He began, *"My beautiful boy, allow me to give you some suggestions to overcome jealousy."*

"How?" I blurted as tears of sadness streamed down my face.

He put my hand in his, said, *"In order to conquer jealousy, you have to know that the person whom you are jealous of has done something good in the past, and now he is reaping the fruit. Therefore, if you release your ego-driven self to the wind, you, too, will one day receive good kismet in return. That my boy, is rule number one.*

"Rule number two: take your jealousy as inspiration to gain merit from Allah.

"Rule number three: create a sense of belonging with the person you are jealous of, and visualize him as an extension of you.

"Rule number four: be grateful for all that you have that he doesn't have. In your case, an example would be your unique education, which only a few have the privilege to experience. You also have a Valet, mentor and chaperone who loves you unconditionally and unceasingly.

"The fifth rule may be difficult, but if you can become friends with your adversary, you'll find that you have a lot more in common than not.

"The sixth rule is to be aware that in the current of time, everything will perish and cease to exist, and this grievous affliction will also pass.

I listened attentively to the physician's sound advice. He promulgated, *"This brings me to rule number seven: remind yourself that at one time or another, he, too, had jealous feelings similar to your own, and understand that all that envy of you has not brought fulfillment in the long haul.*

"Rule number eight is to praise the person you are jealous of superlatively. Remember: what goes around will return to you.

"Always remind yourself that feelings of elation or rejection are temporary; these emotions will soon pass to nothingness. That is rule number nine.

"Rule number ten may be difficult, but one of the best way to overcome jealousy is not to recognize this negative emotion. If you view this negative feeling as your reality, it will energize your ignorance to grow. Sooner or later it will expand to become the monster that you visualize it to be. This negative emotion will dissipate if you do not give it power.

"The final rule is to see your opponent as a passing phase in your mind's eye. Our physical bodies will return to dust sooner or later, and he too will parish. Therefore, don't waste your positive energy by giving strength to the negative forces.

"Last, but not least, is a rule of thumb. If none of the above suggestions work, go for a stroll or sleep it off," my advisor jested flippantly.

My Guardian Angel

While the sheik dished out his rules of subduing the green-eyed-monster, the golden exterior of Kinkaku-ji was lit by the morning sun. The sparkling reflection of the temple on the shimmering pond blinded my eyes. Beams of flaxen rays glistened as if an angelic host had descended from the cloudless sky. My guardian angel had once again manifested in my presence. He beckoned me to his side with outstretched arms before wrapping his gigantic wings around my person. He embraced my spirit, warming my disillusionment with his cozy, feathery down. My disenchantment evaporated. My heart enveloped the purity of his ethos, as he had done a year ago when I had dreamed of him before joining the Enlightened Royal Oracle Society. He whispered now as he did before, *"When you call my name, I will be by your side. I will never abandon you. Do not be afraid. No harm will befall you. Now go and be on your way."*

The angel evanesced as quickly as he had appeared, leaving me in the company of the doctor and the Marquis. Mathieu queried as soon as I had snapped out of my euphoria, *"What's with this boy?"*

Before I could get my bearings, Fahrib had replied on my behalf, *"He is suffering from a case of 'jalousie.'"*

Amused by the doctor's diagnosis, Mathieu queried, *"Dont il est jaloux de (who is he jealous of)?"* The sheik indicated the copulating couple, now passionately weaving around the icon of Bodhisattva Kannon within The Tower of Sound Waves.

The French aristocrat mused, *"I see."*

The Arab dispensed, "Young, a walk in these serene gardens will brighten your spirit and cheer up your soul."

"What an excellent idea! I'll be delighted to keep him company while his chaperone is busy at it," the marquis championed.

I was afraid to be alone with the Frenchman in case he used this opportunity to accost me. I commented importunately, *"I'm not allowed to be out of Andy's sight. He is very strict about this."*

"I'll come with you. I, too, would like to see the grounds of this majestic property," Fahrib remarked.

I was indeed glad that the doctor accompanied us. It was not that I disliked the marquis – it had more to do with my desire to gain the upper hand with this man by holding off his sexual advances for as long as I possible could. At that young age, I already knew the rules of cat and mouse. The further I could stave him off, the more he would covet my affection and the more lavish gifts I would receive from this wealthy aristocrat. This was a secret I did not reveal to anyone, not even to my beloved Andy. His forthrightness would have censured my iniquitous scheme. I was sure my noble Valet would never approve my repugnant stratagem. I was also fully aware that my outward innocence could charm many, and this asset was my weapon to achieving my goals and aspirations. I had yet to conceive that what I put out would eventually return to haunt me.

Ginkaku-ji

This sister pavilion never attained the glory of the Temple of the Golden Pavilion. The creator, Ashikaga Yoshimasa, of Ginkaku-ji (the Silver Pavilion) had planned his retirement villa and gardens as early as 1460. It was after his passing that this extensive property was converted into a Zen temple. The Silver Pavilion sought to emulate the golden Kinkaku-ji, built by Yoshimasa's grandfather, Ashikaga Yoshimitsu. Yoshimasa's initial plan was to cover the exterior with a distinctive silver foil, but due to the onset of the Ōnin War, construction halted.

Similar to Kinkaku-ji, Ginkaku-ji was originally built to serve as a place of rest and solitude for the Shogun. During his reign, Shogun Ashikaga Yoshimasa inspired a new outpouring of traditional culture, which came to be known as Higashiyama Bunka (the

Culture of the Eastern Mountain). Having retired to the villa, it was rumored that Yoshimasa sat in the pavilion, contemplating the serenity and beauty of the gardens as the war worsened and Kyoto burned to the ground.

It was here that the three of us sat to contemplate the eternal beauty of the unfinished Temple of the Silver Pavilion, officially known as Jishō-ji, the Temple of Shining Mercy. The abundance of varieties of mosses and the 'Mount Fuji' sand garden within the inner courtyard garnered an emotional poignancy within me.

Tears filled my eyes once again. This time, they were droplets of joy. I was weeping at the grandeur of Allah's dazzling magnificence, crafted by the hands of men. As the abundance of reddish-golden maple leaves flickered onto the yellow earth, serendipity washed over my being.

The advice the learned physician had so eloquently expressed earlier had made perfect sense. A sense of bromance for Fahrib took hold of me. Unexpectedly, I reached over and planted a lingering kiss on Fahrib's lips. Astonished by my unanticipated action, the marquis looked on in amazement. The sheik, taken by surprise, was as bewildered as our companion. He did not know how to react to my sudden, impassioned outburst. Before he could utter a word, I imbedded another kiss on the doctor's lips. He did not withdraw. Instead, our lips stayed locked in a passionate embrace.

I, for one, did not know what had come over me. Neither did the Arab. Neither of us pulled away until the marquis forged a fraudulent cough, *"Uhh Hmmm!"* he voiced phlegmatically. *"I'm still here, boys. Do you need a moment to yourselves?"*

We pulled away instantaneously. I did not know how to respond to that remark. Fahrib did the talking: *"That won't be necessary. I think we should be heading back to join our entourage."*

We prattled on much about nothing on our journey back to the golden pavilion. By then, the Arab and I had already forged an unspoken bond that only the two of us could chronicle in our implicit lives' journals.

Before I was called upon to take position in the *Chamber of Dharma Waters* for my *Sacred Sex in Sacred Places* session with Guy and Yuri, my jealousy of Keiko had miraculously vanished. In its place was veneration and reverence for the young man and my Valet. As per the sheik's advice, I had made it a point to befriend Keiko. True to Fahrib's advice, the Eurasian also possessed jealousy and envy like everyone else. As he had mentioned, every one of us is harnessed by an unseen connecting thread, and that is the cosmic order of the human race. Keiko was indeed not just an extension of me, but of all humanity.

SMALL GESTURES

by

Cleo Scornavacca

"We will forever be known by the tracks we leave"

- A Native American Proverb

To my husband Sal and our daughter Nikki

It was in 1998 when I found myself faced with possibly the greatest challenge of my life at that point. We all have had obstacles in our lives that negatively affected us at one time or another. Yet, when it's something that you can't predict, nor have any control over once it has hit you, it's by far more devastating.

That was exactly what happened to me.

We moved into our first home in the early summer of 1996. It was perfect. A hidden little treasure in the middle of suburban New Jersey. The home was described in print as a "sprawling ranch" that rested on a tree-lined acre of land. The realtor went on to say that the yard was secluded and park-like. After seeing the property, my husband and I couldn't have agreed more, so we bought it.

We settled in and did what most people do when they buy a new home. We put our personal stamp on it and made it our own. We painted, decorated the walls with my husband's artwork, planted flowerbeds, a vegetable garden and even more trees. My husband put up a fence to make the yard a safer place for our four year old daughter and our four year old Doberman Pinscher to run and play in.

Like many families, we were busy at our day jobs. At the time, I was working as a make-up artist and commuting at least an hour one way to my job each day. It wasn't anything out of the ordinary, most people did the same thing in their everyday lives.

About two years after living in the house, I started to not feel well. I was tired all the time, but I dismissed it. I chalked it up to long hours at work and being burnt out. I promised myself that I would rest on my days off and I convinced myself that my plan to take it easy would balance out my workdays.

That well-rested feeling never came. I didn't go to the doctor, because I was just too busy. I had anemia during my adolescence, so I further justified my state of ill-health by saying I needed to be more diligent about taking my vitamins. I did do just that, but it was to no avail. I still didn't feel any better. In fact, I was feeling worse.

It finally came to a head in October of that year. I was driving home from my mother-in-law's house in Northern New Jersey after picking up our daughter, when I started to feel strange. I remember that it was dark and the rain was heavy that evening. The highway was crowded, which had made me even more anxious. My daughter was seated in the back of the car, as she vividly described her day at Grandma's in a way that only a child could, when I suddenly felt like I was going to pass out. I had enough sense of mind to pull over and call home. Yet no one answered. I then called my brother, who came for us.

He wanted to take me to the hospital, but I again thought I was just stressed out and over worked, so I told him no and with that he brought us to our parent's home. That way I wouldn't be alone being that my husband hadn't returned home from work yet.

Once there, I had to lie down. And once I did, it was there that I stayed for the next week. I had developed a headache that was unlike anything I had ever felt before and I couldn't lift my head up off the pillow. It was just too hard. My husband brought me to the doctor and they couldn't find anything wrong. They said it might possibly be a severe sinus infection and gave me medication. Yet, the headache wouldn't subside. It had actually gotten worse.

I finally went to the hospital and after a slew of tests, they diagnosed me with Lyme Disease. The test numbers indicated that I had it for quite some time and what I had been feeling in the months past were the effects of the disease being left untreated. I had heard many horror stories of the damage that the disease had done to people who weren't diagnosed in the early stages. I was scared. I knew that if the past weeks were any example of what life would be like in the future, it could be very serious and it was something that I was not willing to accept. But what could I do to make myself better?

At first, I felt sorry for myself. Then I got angry. I wondered how I had gotten it in the first place. I didn't remember a tick bite or a rash that would have sent up a red flag. Then I began to worry about how much damage the disease might have already done. It was all a vicious circle. I wanted to get better, but how? Then one day my answer came. It came in the form of a small gesture, a gesture from my little girl.

I was lying in my hospital bed after being admitted due to my diagnosis and my symptoms. At that time, they didn't deal with Lyme Disease the way they do today, so I had to stay for further testing and medication. My husband came every day after work with our daughter.

This one specific day was Halloween. Our daughter came dressed in her Halloween costume that I had purchased weeks before. She sat on my bed and told me about her day, in between giggling and hunting through her goodie bag for candy. I didn't envy my husband that evening. She was six years old and was loaded up with sugar. It was going to be a long night for him.

After some time, they said goodnight and told me that they would be back tomorrow. When they left the room I had a sinking feeling in the pit of my stomach. My eyes burned and I started to cry. I didn't want to cry in front of our daughter. She was already dealing with too much at her age by seeing her mommy in the hospital. I didn't want her to be frightened, so I saved my tears for after they left.

On that particular evening, the curtains to the window in my hospital room were still open. My room was on the first floor and it overlooked the visitors parking lot. I hadn't realized it before, but for some odd reason I noticed it then.

As I stared out the window, I saw my husband and my daughter on the sidewalk outside. They were illuminated by the street light above them. They were waiting to cross the street, so they could go to the car and drive home. I sat up straight and I noticed that my husband pointed out where my room was. They were just about to cross the street to the lot when our daughter turned, lifted her tiny hand and gave me a small wave. I waved back hoping that she saw me. Then she looked up at her dad, smiled and put that little hand of hers in his and they walked away.

That's when I knew I had to get better, no matter what. I saw that picture of just the two of them and it was missing something. It was missing me. I couldn't let this illness make me weaker and make me miss out on the important things in life. I needed to be the person holding her other hand while she crossed the street. I needed to take better care of myself. I needed to recognize the warning signs of stress, of illness or of just being overworked and not ignore them. I needed to put me and my family first.

When I came home at the end of that week, I started to read up on Lyme Disease, the good, the badly and the ugly. I started to read up on wellness and how it applied to me. I had a great deal of crippling muscle pain at the time. I had read somewhere that yoga was very helpful for many in my situation, but I was just too tired to do it. Plus I was on intravenous antibiotics for the treatment of my disease stage, so exercise would have been awkward. In addition, I was told to stay in bed and rest. It was all very frustrating for me.

Then I had an idea. What if I did the yoga in bed? I was extremely weak. Even taking a shower would require me to go back to bed to rest, but I thought if I do just a little each day, I had to feel better than I felt at the time. My husband agreed and stated there was something he needed to do, as well.

When we had originally bought the house there was an attached deck in the back that had a ramp instead of steps. The former owner's wife was in a wheelchair and needed the ramp so she was able to go out onto the lawn. My husband saw this as a bad omen, so he sat down and said to me that he was going to rip out the ramp. He said there was no reason for it. No one here needed it to get into the yard. And with that, he used the wood to raise the boards to make the deck level and added a step down to the lawn…another small gesture.

Eventually, I did get better six months later. I went back to work and realized, as cliche as this may sound, it's the little things…the small gestures. The positive things that others did that helped me and made all the difference.

We all need them, it's so important. It's what supports us and gives us strength. Maybe even that little push to keep going. Whether it's something we do for someone we know or even a stranger. It's bigger than the gesture itself. Even the little things we do for ourselves make our lives full, whole.

If you take anything away from this story it's this, remember to make your day the best it can be. It doesn't have to be something grandiose, it just has to come from the heart. Smile at a stranger, hold the door for someone else. Say good morning. Carry groceries for a person that may need help. Give someone a hug that could use it. Have coffee with a friend, laugh, cry, whatever. Make time for those you love. Take a moment and just do it.

Take time for yourself, as well. Go for a walk on the beach or in the park. Play with your pets. Read a good book. Listen to music. Paint a picture. Have a warm cup of something soothing and watch the snow fall or the sun set, spend an hour or spend a minute, if that's all the time you have in your day? Just step outside your door. You don't have to go far. Stand there and take a deep breath in, whether it be in the coolest of the morning or the stillness of dark. Be quiet and listen, even if it's only for that moment. Enjoy that time you have for those small, precious things. Those gestures that seem to get lost throughout our busy days.

Today, I hope that my story is one of those things… this is my small gesture to you.

SYMPHONY

by

JD Stockholm

She could still hear it, even though he was gone, the symphony of their time together, and the way he played with such passion. She missed him so much, but she had made him a promise, never stop dancing, never fade into the shadows. She vowed she never would. She'd held his hand as he took his last breath, reached her fingers out to trace his hairline. Even in death he was so beautiful.

Her heart threatened to split with an emptiness nothing would ever be fill. After he had been laid to rest, she had stayed behind. Just sat and watched him. Listening to the sound of music the world would never hear again, but she could. It was in her soul. He had put it there.

She kicked off her shoes. Closed her eyes and let his music flow through her. She swayed at first, just in time, but then, she felt his arms around her, felt his chin resting upon her shoulder from behind. "I'll never leave you," he whispered. "For as long as you walk this earth, so will I."

They danced.

THE BUTTERFLY GIRL

by

Linda Hamonou

"If the butterfly wings its way to the sweet light that attracts it, it's only because it doesn't know that the fire can consume it."

- Giordano Bruno

To my godmother.

1

The day I met her was the day I fell.

I can't run, because... Add your reasons! Look at me, add one! Come on, you know you want to. What are you afraid of? Everybody does it!

All right then, let me help you.

"Randy, you have to stop, your heart won't hold!"

I'm running. It's not even that I did it on purpose. I'm five and all the kids are running, so I might do it too. Except that I'm not like all the kids.

My mother grabs me by the hand and lower herself next to me so that she can look into my eyes. Her eyes are blue, like the sky above.

"Randy, you can't do that. You know you can't."

I look down because I know it, she and my dad repeat it all the time. No running, no climbing the stairs without a break every three steps, no playing outside if they are not watching me, no walking too far. I know it, and I hate it. I want to run, not because I want to be normal, because I want to be special, but the other kind of special though, the kind who wins the Marathon.

Seriously, I don't even remember how that idea came to my head or when, but here it is and it's not going anywhere.

You see the problem? My heart can't take it. Genetic malformation, I have some weird noise in there. Not that I really care though.

Skip forward a few years, we need to get back to how I met her.

2

I'm running again. I'm not on the track team, 'cause I can't, obviously. That doesn't stop me from running. I help Josie to climb over the gate. It's cold and slippery because it has been raining, and the rusty paint is coming out more than usual, I hate having that stuff on my hands.

Josie sits in the covered part of the bench and prepares her cigarette. She rolls them because she says it's healthier, just tobacco not all the garbage the cigarette companies put in. But I know that's bullshit, she just wants to add some pot in there. I don't really care. I don't smoke, my mum would kill me, if the smoke doesn't kill me first. Damn, she would kill me if she knew I'm running too.

I get to the tracks and start preparing. I know it's going to be hard today because the ground is muddy and clinging to my shoes.

I run.

I feel fine really. I'm good at it too. All right, I'm not going to win the Marathon tomorrow but hey, I'm still running. The first lap is all right. The second is a bit harder but it's always harder. At first, that's when I would stop and then I would hate myself for it because I thought it was my limit, until the day I decided to force pass through. Best day of my life!

My chest burns.

Then the third lap, the burning is almost over, once I'm done there, I know I'll be all right. Four, five. Josie is stroking her hands against each other because of the cold. She doesn't wear her gloves when she smokes, she says she would catch fire. Her face is almost hidden by her long blond hair but I know she is looking at me intensely, just in case.

My knee refuses to fold. I laugh because my heart is fine, because it's not my heart screwing with me, it's all the rest. One step, another one and the ground is rushing towards me, all the wet little grey stones in the sand and I can't even rise my hands to protect my face because my arms won't work either.

I fell.

3

Josie totally panicked. Ambulance, my mom, the hospital. They said that my heart was still holding but that they had to keep me in for a few days. Just to do more tests. It happens once in a while, not a big deal, except for my mum. She almost wanted to stay with me but I told her to go back to work and to get Josie home. Falling on my face was already embarrassing enough.

The nurse walks in front of me in the corridor. They have drawings on the walls, probably made by the kids who stay here longer than me. The place is too quiet though, a place full of children should be in chaos but I guess none of them have the energy to come and run in the corridor. The nurse opens a door and waits until we are in the middle of the room to say anything.

"Hi Alex, you are going to have a friend for a while."

Alex stands at the wall, brush in hand. She glances at me from head to toes above her shoulder.

"You're a guy," she says stating the obvious.

Mind you, I wasn't sure that she was a girl. She was wearing the uni-gender white gown, they put on you whenever you need to do serious stuff, she had an IV attached to her left hand that rested on the bed and well, she had no hair.

"It's just for a few days," the nurse says. "You can paint some butterflies for him if you want, his name is Randy."

The nurse points at the other bed further away from the window and I don't realize when I move toward it. I'm still staring at Alex.

"So you're not dying?" Alex asks.

"I'm not sure yet," I say.

I mean we are all dying just, with different speed and sometimes you have more reasons to die. But truthfully at that moment, I didn't know what was wrong with me.

"Nobody is dying," the nurse says a little bit too cheerfully.

Alex glares at her, she is definitely having none of it. Then she sighs, shakes her head and goes back to color her pencil drawn butterfly on the wall with paint.

"You can't catch a butterfly if you're not dying, so make up your mind," she says.

She isn't even looking at me so I don't answer. I take off my shoes and climb on the bed, hoping they aren't going to give me a white gown, because more than sharing a room with a girl, being half naked doing it would be embarrassing.

"Someone will come get you later for the tests," the nurse says and she leaves me alone with Alex.

4

"The last one who came here, she died before she could catch her butterfly." Alex says, "but it won't happen to me, I'm getting out of here."

Alex puts her brush down in a glass of water and turns to me. The way she looks at me gave me the chill, it is as if she is trying to decide if I am going to die and how long it is going to take.

"I'm getting out of here too, I have a Marathon to run."

She sits on her bed. She has dozens of butterflies flying around her, painted on the wall in different colors.

"So you're definitely not dying then," she says as if she is a little bit disappointed.

"Not yet," I say.

She turns on the other side and grabs a book.

I wasn't dying, so I wasn't interesting for her anymore. You see, Alex was... Alex had leukaemia. But Alex couldn't die because she had a plan. A way better plan than my poor training plan for the Marathon, Alex was getting out of here, literally.

She never really sleeps, at least that was what she says. She never closes her eyes either which made me believe her at first. It is freaky. She stares at the ceiling all eyes opened. I know she is sleeping because her breathing is so slow and when she isn't sleeping she is either painting or reading. She spends the night like that, all eyes opened. Some of the nurses try to get her eyes to close from time to time but she always opens them right back, as if she is afraid that closing them would take her away before she has found the right butterfly.

It's her theory. That the butterflies carry the soul of the dead away but she doesn't believe in spirituality, I'm not even sure she believes in souls either, she believes in weird science. And she has made up her mind that she can travel from one body to the next in a parallel universe if she follows the right butterfly in her mind.

5

"So what did you dream about?" She asks one morning at breakfast.

Breakfast isn't a fun time. It never stays inside of her and she repeats that she doesn't need food but she still eats it all, maybe to keep me company.

"I told you, I never dream and if I do I never remember a thing."

"You dream or you'll be dead."

"Then you sleep or you'll be dead."

"I am dying which means that my needs are different than yours. I don't sleep, I travel to other places. Last night I was in an hospital just like this one except Julie wasn't dead yet, but I was way worse. That freaked me out."

Julie is the girl who was in my bed before. I'm still not sure how I feel about sharing the bed of a dead girl, especially that I was supposed to be here for a few days and it has already been a week.

"But that's what you are trying to do, right? Find a universe like this one and hijack your other self's body."

I told you that sounded crazy.

"Yeah, but not one where I'll die too, that would be pointless."

"But you came back, how do you intend to stay there? When you find the place?"

"I'll just have to catch my butterfly," Alex answered.

Then she starts coughing, presses the button to call the nurse and slides out of bed. I turn to look at the wall. I tried to help her once but she doesn't really appreciate my help.

"It's not your job, you are here to make sure I catch the butterflies," she said and she pushed me away crawling to the bathroom her legs unable to carry her.

At least, I know the feeling, that is the reason why I'm here and since I arrived my body has stopped reacting a few times already, for no apparent reasons. I want to bet on another weird genetic disorder but they'll test everything they can think of before making that leap.

Alex manages to get to the bathroom by herself before she even vomits anything, it is better than most days.

6

The butterfly Alex has drawn on the wall this morning is a lot brighter than the others around it. It is more colorful. She has had a night butterflies series that I can see and she never wants to mention what they really mean or where they come from. The new one is pink and purple with a bit of blue and light green on the side of the wings, not really like any real butterfly I have ever seen. Still something seems to be missing from one wing, a slightly grey spot.

The nurses arrive to take care of Alex. There is not talking to her for the rest of the morning so I put my earphones on, not to listen to her being taken away. I try to think about something else, but every time I close my eyes, all I can see is the new butterfly and what it really means. When she manages to fill that grey spot with color, she will be gone forever, I'm sure of it.

"Where is she?"

If there is one person to freak out more than my mum, that is definitely Alex's mum. I think I can understand, every time she walks out of here she isn't sure her daughter will be here when she comes back.

"They took her upstairs," I say.

She throws me the dark look she reserves especially for me.

Dying is competition in her mind. Every single girl who shared the room with Alex died and somehow it seems to me that her mother considers that a victory.

"He is not dying," was the first thing Alex said about me when her mother first visited and I could see she hated me for it, as if I was now the one winning over death in this competition.

"She wasn't supposed to go before this afternoon," Alex's mother says.

She places a new bunch of paint tubes on Alex's bed. Better, brighter colors for the butterflies, I notice and it scares me a little.

Don't they know that if Alex catches her real butterfly we will never see here again? Apparently, they aren't taking her seriously.

7

All right, I wasn't taking her seriously either, I mean she sounded crazy most of the time but still so rationally crazy that I had my doubts.

But "where is she?" is the question I'll be asking myself for the rest of my life.

I don't know what they do to her when they take her upstairs. It happened three times while I'm there and every time she comes down, she seems even sicker than before and I never thought that was possible. I can see her cheekbones through her transparent skin. Then she raves about butterflies until she makes herself sick.

This last time, she doesn't.

The sun is already down when she comes back and she has missed the 5pm dinner. Her mother holds her hand for long after passed visit time. Alex is only laughing and coughing a lot and unable to keep any food in so she doesn't even bother after her two first spoonfuls.

I wake up sweating in the middle of the night. The room is hot, I feel like I'm on fire. Alex is lying on the bed, her eyes closed and that throws me in a panic. I press the nurses call button so many times that it probably just ends up ignoring me.

I wait seconds that feel like hours, stand up on cotton legs to go to Alex. When I take her hand, it's so cold that I can't hang on to it. Maybe it's her, maybe it's my fever, I can't tell.

I think I'm going to vomit that green stuff that keeps on coming out of her after every meal. I walk to the corridor and one of the nurse grabs me.

"Something is wrong with Alex, something... her eyes, I can't see her eyes..."

The nurse probably think I'm crazy because she just smiles at me, tell me I must have had a bad dream, that she is going to check on my fever, that I need to get back to bed, all that sort of hospital nonsense.

She opens the door, helping me back in as I cling to the wall for support.

Alex is gone.

There are butterflies dancing on the top of her bed in the wavering light coming from the corridor, but Alex isn't here, and the butterflies she had painted are gone too. Just I'm the only one who notice.

8

"Come on Randy, you can do this!"

A voice in the crowd that I haven't heard for years. Of course, my parents aren't here, they thought it was folly. Why would I of all people try to run the Marathon?

"Come on Randy! You're not dead yet!"

That voice, her voice.

I turned to look everywhere but I can't see her face.

The place is full of people with numbers on, like me, the runners. And on the side, behind the ropes, people watching us, anonymous.

The race started.

Then on my shoulder, a butterfly, pink and purple with a bit of blue and light green on the side of the wings and the certainty that this is the world where we both got to live.

INSPIRATION

by

Naomi Shaw

Dedicated to Krystie

Inspiration

In the times you feel invisible
Like chains are tying you down
Just lift your head up to the sky
That way it's impossible to frown.

No matter what, you are just beautiful
And nothing can take your beauty away
Keep searching for the light in the tunnel
Just make sure you look the right way.

God has a special reason for everyone
You may not have discovered it yet.
He loves every one of his children
Have faith, because He will never forget.

Remember, the sun shines for you
It rises each and every day
So open your heart let the love in
And inspiration will find a way

So when outside it is stormy weather
And it's painful to move with the pain
Close your eyes and with a little imagination
You'll be dancing in the rain

MY LOSS

by

S.L. Bull

"Life's destination is not what brings us happiness, but the journey to get there."

- Dan Millman

My name is S.L. Bull. I am a mother of 3 beautiful daughters, but I have also experience the loss of an unborn child. I was 4 weeks along when I found out I was pregnant. My husband and I were trying to have a son and were excited because I had a feeling that we were finally having our boy. We have always gone off of what I felt we were having since it hasn't steered us wrong so this was a big deal.

As soon as I found out I made all the phone calls to the doctors to start scheduling appointments and getting everything started for the pregnancy. It was an exciting time for us, even more so then before. What we didn't know was that in just a few short weeks things would change and we would face a horror that we thought would never happen to us.

At 6 weeks along my morning sickness had started to subside, which was strange so I called my doctor and they said it could come and go so it was nothing to really worry about. So I didn't worry and kept doing what I was doing. A few days later I started to have some spotting and then it stopped so I thought it was the normal implantation spotting from the egg attaching to my uterus walls. I had no idea it was the start of something worse.

Just 2 days after the spotting it started again. Only this time it didn't stop but slowly got heavier as the morning progressed. My husband was at work so I was at home with the 2 of our children who are not yet in school. By the time mid-morning came around I decided it was time to go to the emergency room to make sure everything was ok.

I was scared as I had a horrible feeling something was wrong and had to be there by myself. My mother had showed up to watch the girls so she couldn't even go with me. After 3 hours of tests and an ultrasound the ER doctor finally came into my room. He told me I was having a miscarriage at 7 weeks and there was nothing that could be done. My worst fear had come true. I was experiencing the loss of a child. I know most don't see it that way, but to me it was the loss of a child we had already accepted and wanted and loved just as much as the rest. My world crashed around me. I was in shock and couldn't even cry at that moment. He must have asked me several times if I was ok and all I could do was nod my head. When he finally gave me my release papers and left the room I broke down. I sat there and cried for 30 minutes before I could leave and drive myself home.

When I got home I broke down even more. My mom held me as I cried for hours until I realized I needed to go tell my husband that we would not be having the little boy we had hoped for after all. I put my 2 girls in the car, picked up the other from school early and headed to his work. When I told him he was in a state of shock and didn't even know what to say or do other than hug me, but it was just the beginning.

The next few days I detached myself from everything and everyone including my husband. He did the same, but not to the extent I did. I didn't even want to be in a room with my other children. I just wanted to be left alone. I was ready to give up. I had lost a child and didn't realize that the others still needed me. It almost ruined my marriage, my kids were in an uproar and unsure if their parents love them, my family was fighting with me every time I turned around. I felt as if the world had finally turned against me and it was the end. I never saw an end to any of it. It was like this for weeks before my mother told me somethings she had learned over the years and after losing children (4 of them) herself.

She said that during our darkest hours we can realize how strong we really are and keep fighting. We know in our hearts that we are not given something in life that we cannot handle and that everything has a purpose no matter how bad it may seem. It is our love for our families, friends, and even the occasional stranger that gives us a simple smile as they walk by that give this world hope and a brighter future. Find something to hold onto that makes you happy and turn to those simple things during your time of need and you will find a certain level of comfort in them to help you through anything.

These are the words everyone needs to hear. We all need to push through our tough times and come back stronger than before. Life is too precious to let anything tear you down. Fight back and remember that we are never alone in our battles. Someone is always there to help us through them. We just have to let them in so they can help and give us the support we need when we need it most.

My pain has not gone away, but it is much easier for me to deal with and I now look at the positive side of things. Without dealing with this loss I would have never been able to help my brother with his when he lost his son. I would not have been able to comfort a teen age girl in my town when she lost her baby, but most of all I would have never known how strong I could be and how much my family and friends needed me when I pulled away.

Keep your head up. Find the light in the darkness and shine brighter when you know everything around you is trying to snuff out your fire. We owe it to ourselves to brave this cruel world and show them what we are made of and that we will not break no matter what is thrown at us. We are strong, brave, and loved. That is what the world needs to know and see.

This is my story and I hope you find the light!

BREATHE IN ME

by

Siren X Star

"Scar tissue is stronger than regular tissue. Realize the strength. Move on."

- Henry Rollins

Dedicated to all of us who keep fighting.

Breathe in Me

The haze covers the mountains
In front of you

As autumn leaves fall
From the weeping trees
Littering the path in beauty

The creek's voice calming & soothing
As you take the first step
On your own path

Let the light of the sun embrace you
Let the fire burn in you

Ignite the passion once fleeting
As you live & breathe this beautiful existence

Renew you
Renew the spark

Create your own path from your heart
And keep moving forward

RAGING SILENCE

by

Pablo Michaels

When silence rage in your heart, express your affection and love for who or what causes your silence. You will discover your silence and rage within is nothing but your passion for life and your part in the universe.

He sat on a deck chair outside a house far out in rural Moraga, after lunch at a silent yoga retreat with reservations about remaining silent, all day. He appreciated the bees flying around him and the others at the yoga retreat; he viewed them as keepers of peace, sharing this retreat with friends, who were all joined in the human spirit as seekers of the fleeting moment of eternal life, love, joy, peace, and light. He climbed a mountain, finding peace, a source of light, even though silence remained in his soul.

He observed the same brilliant, shining light with all his friends at this retreat and with the bees. He originally had reservations of participating in the retreat, since when silence raged, it had been his place of isolation which brought depression and psychosis. Silence had always been his worst enemy. Why his enemy? He hid and ran from his feelings, retreating to solitude. He sensed his rage inside and the inadequacy of knowing how to express the brewing storm of anger about his identity. He did not know how to channel his silence about his emotions in a peaceful process. A few memories, suggestions, and processes from the past helped him walk the path to recovery, finding peace. He learned when silence raged in his heart to express his affection and love to what and who caused his silence. He discovered his silence and rage within was nothing but his passion for life and his part in the universe.

During the yoga session in the morning, Shandi, the yoga guru, led each asana together with them at their own individual levels. They practiced the earth in its peace, slowly and carefully, with each pose, stretch, and breath. With Trikonasana (the triangle), savasana (deep relaxation and meditation), the sounds of prana (cleansing breathing), and the yoga mudra (the yoga energy seal), they joined together in the spirit of peace.

Eating a vegetarian lunch without words spoken, they were all together.

The time arrived for the Buddhist chants and songs with various musical instruments. They sang and made music. They visualized a higher plane of understanding of the universe. They are part of that and pay homage to it, loudly singing with their souls to be heard.

After the musical experience, they went on a meditational walk. The students followed the leader, synchronized by stepping in unison behind each other in silence, walking, together in a steady trance of tranquility through the wooded hillsides and pastures, where horses grazed.

He visualized the light coming from the spirit of doing with others with care, not as a solitary, lonely moment. Times of silence were not a disease or isolation; they were times of peace. Enlightened, silence to him meant a moment to express what was inside; peace, rage, love, sorrow, joy, anger, happiness, ignorance, and knowledge, which was easy for all to express.

When the silent yoga retreat ended he knew Om, Shanti, Om, was the process for, love, joy, light, and knowledge, as the vehicle to peace. Driving home, he glanced at the green chaparral and oak covered hills. The scene reminded him of a time from his past.

In the fall of 1966, when he left home to study at California Polytechnic College in San Luis Obispo, which by most people referred to as Cal Poly, he lay on a lounge chair, outside his apartment, The Islander. By the swimming pool, with the sun blazing warmly on his body, he contemplated his homework and studies, while watching with careful glances the trim, muscular bodies of other male students. But his observations remained silent. He worried if his roommates discovered his attraction to men, they would ridicule him at the very least. They told fag jokes, frequently, especially about obvious gay boys in high school. He shuttered at the very thought of being the brunt of one of their humiliations. He grew a mustache and becoming brown skinned from continuous tanning, all the while dreaming of how to change his life, searching for something, not exactly sure what it was. Still, he felt the seeds of peace germinating inside him, and tried to practice his life accordingly.

His roommates and friends nicknamed him Pablo; the reason why they chose this name escaped him. Pablo felt the birth of a new life in his blood, and instinctively knew times were changing, with world-wide peace and love for all humanity dawning. Some of his changes hid deeper in his heart, soul, and loins, but still his thoughts remained silent and alone.

That winter it rained so much, the hillside outside the apartment came sliding down into the swimming pool, which caused the water to swell up to his front door.

.That spring the sun shone for brief periods between rain storms. The weathered, worn slopes of the volcano, ascending above their apartment, burst out with the colors of a vibrant, yellow from the wild mustard and the emerald sheen of the glistening, green grass, covering the mountain slopes. This mountain was one of nine volcanos between San Luis Obispo and Morro Rock in Morrow Bay, the mountains, aptly named the Mountains of Fire. The bright green grass, appearing iridescent, reminded him of the psychedelic light shows at the Fillmore Auditorium and the Avalon Ballroom, where he, his roommates, and friends from high school used to spend time together, listening to the Jefferson Airplane, Quicksilver, and the Grateful Dead with Pigpen.

Pablo began smoking cigarettes in those early college days to remind him of the elevated mood of the music, creating a sense of belonging with the other people smoking grass. He gradually became addicted to nicotine. Through smoking cigarettes, he identified with other people who wanted to change the country and the world as it existed. Smoking became a socialized habit similar to the practice of peace pipe smoking done by native, American Indians, long before.

His four roommates, Russell, Lenny, Sloop, Chester, and Pablo migrated to Cal Poly from their home room high school class. They roomed together in two apartments in the Islander, an apartment complex, housing the male students. They ate their meals in the Tropicana Apartments across the creek, where the women lived. Russ, Lenny, and Pablo majored in architecture, while Chester chose engineering, and Sloop pursued a career in physical therapy and education. Russ, the true artist amongst them, had painted an abstract picture of all five roommates in a boat. The fresco, depicting a puzzle of the men, kept them wondering about Russ's interpretation of their lives and futures. It hung above the turquoise couch in the small living room, carpeted with a loud orange shag. A white, popcorn textured the ceiling, typical of the boxed, nineteen sixties architectural designed buildings.

Most of the boys allowed their hair to grow longer. They listened to Chester strumming his guitar with the folk songs of Bob Dylan, Donovan, and Joan Baez popular with those seeking a new world order. Chester's life was destined to new beginnings with the guitar and sitar along with their intricate, Eastern influence. Lenny shared his John Handy albums, jazz of the saxophone with its mellow digressions into complex variations of melodies. Pablo worshipped Simon and Garfunkel's music, especially the lyrics to their album, *Parsley, Rosemary, Rage, and Thyme.* They became his anthems for his attempts to write poetry and the beginnings of stories about their collegiate relationships and pursuits in love. Simon and Garfunkel brought out his long, hidden emotions of romance and love for nature. But he realized their thoughts and emotions were not his own. So, he began to write to express own his inner self, transforming his inner rage and silence into words.

Many people came to visit in their humble but modern living arrangement. High school friends from other colleges, hitch-hiking Highway 101, stopped to rest and regain strength, building deeper friendships on their journeys to meet other friends at different destinations. This companionship lasted into future years.

Many love interests of feminine persuasion passed through their front and bedroom doors that fall and winter. They met two young girls, both named Madonna. Long, blonde hair draped down sexy Madonna's shoulders. She acquired her nickname, Mystic Madonna, from her eyes, as blue as the ocean. The white foam of waves rolled around the turquoise temptation that lured her followers. She kept all five men hoping she would share her cosmic secrets of love, spinning all their hearts into a web. She never revealed who she would eventually choose as her closest lover. With all courting her, she bounced around to each roommate like a dragonfly, only Sloop withheld, still yearning for his girlfriend back in Berkeley. Madonna's magic shone mostly in her eyes, the roommates falling victim to her mysteriousness. When she was confronted with more serious intentions, she retreated, seeking adventure with another person. Pablo's interest was strictly platonic. They bonded, thinking they understood what really was going on inside each other, a secret they kept to themselves.

Fat Madonna, not that pretty and fairly stout with kinky brown hair and small round eyes, introduced Pablo more into the underground music of the San Francisco Sound. She acquired her knowledge, writing articles for Rolling Stone Magazine. She desired Pablo for more than simply a boyfriend but soon relented. They bonded as friends. One weekend, they hitch-hiked to San Francisco. She introduced him to Chet Helms, the originator and owner of The Family Dog at the Avalon Ballroom. He gave them free admission to the ballroom. Upon entering the club, Janis Joplin with Big Brother and the Holding Company wailed their souls so intently that they both got an immediate high. The exalting pleasure blended with the fragrant smoke of pot and the hovering scent of patchouli oil. Flower children danced, swaying under the strobe lights to the music of Janis Joplin. Behind the musicians, abstract, changing, colored lights and pictures illuminated the wall. Pablo stared at the men, with lustful desires. Another man raged inside. He wanted to dance freely as part of the crowd but felt restrained.

Hitch-hiking back to Cal Poly, Pablo felt strong urges swelling inside him, but he suppressed them deeper within.

Slick, another girl with long black hair, as dark as coal and eyes to match, also had an interest in Pablo. Her skin was as pure and white as freshly fallen snow. But her face barely expressed any emotion, when she spoke. Pablo detected a faint light, sparkling in her eyes, begging him to rescue her from a woeful sorrow, deep within her. But he became distressed with his own identity, many thoughts swirling through his mind. He did not know how to process them, even discuss them with her or anyone else. Unable to tell her that he was not attracted to her, in fear of breaking a shared platonic friendship. He dreamed of meeting a robust male character like from tales of ancient Greece.

One night in delusion, Pablo went for a lengthy walk through the streets of town, until he pounded on the church doors of the Mission in San Luis Obispo. There was no answer within. With the doors locked, voices raged, incoherently inside him. Returning to his apartment, he stopped on the top of the freeway overpass, contemplating throwing his body over the side, in a fleeting moment of desperation. No visions of Michelangelo's gods appeared to help him through his plight, with only his silence and the hum of the traffic, speeding by below. There was no one he could talk to. He continued his walk back to the Islander.

One night shortly after, he met with a fast, thrill-seeking girl, Trixie. Appearing so spontaneously beautiful, she introduced him to her friend, Bob, who was the local supplier of grass. Bob lived upstairs from Pablo's apartment, making it an easy, convenient stroll. They both encouraged him to experience the mind expanding feeling of love by smoking a joint of Bob's current shipment. With his mind and emotions perplexed, he had no reservations about trying something new. He thought it might ignite his mind's vision into a new and different world in which he might be free. Although he smoked cigarettes, the pungent burst of the heavy, marijuana fumes inside his lungs caused him to burst out with a choking embarrassment.

Suddenly his thoughts and observations became distorted, enough to warrant his exit from Bob's apartment without Trixie. Unable to speak, with his thoughts running rampant, even though mildly attracted to Bob, he sensed the spark of a love involvement between Bob and Trixie. He struggled with his balance walking down the stairs. He heard a loud, crashing sound of glass that overwhelmed his senses.

He started walking across the bridge over the creek to visit Slick in the Tropicana Apartments. He had previously planned to visit her. He listened to the conversation of two men passing by. "That guy trying to escape from his girlfriend's apartment, and ran right through the closed glass door. He shattered the glass." No male students were allowed in the women's rooms.

Paranoid and distorted by the effects of the grass, Pablo looked at his hands, arms, and legs, imagining he had smashed through the glass partition. He imagined his whole body dripped with blood. He panicked, thinking he would explain his absence to Slick another time. He had to survive what he currently felt. He ran back to his apartment bedroom. He shut the door and hid beneath the covers of his bed for the duration of the night, in silence, unable to study, remembering only he had missed his date with Slick.

Slick continued to seek his amorous affection. Sadly unable to offer his body for her love, and not having the guts or fortitude to tell her that he craved a man's body, he only recognized the confused silence raging inside him.

Fortunately, one of Pablo's roommates, Lenny, befriended her, healing that episode. When she had slashed her wrists, in a state of depression and confusion, Lenny consoled her feminine melancholy state, ultimately wooing her as his lover. Pablo felt that night, when he was distressed about the shattered glass, imagining his body soaked in blood, he had sent Slick into desperation, driving her to slash her wrists. He felt worse about being unable to surrender his body to her sensual passions to make love.

These low feelings passing through their lives coincided with all their short personal entanglements, with intimacy much too brief for any sustainable growth. Some of their intimate relationships occurred with too much intensity; others who were divided by distance, like Sloop and his girlfriend, who attended Cal in Berkeley. But all these friendships, relationships, and events formed the foundation of made Pablo.

Pablo smoked grass with Trixie and Bob again, on the bridge over the creek between the Tropicana and the Islander, not staying long and walking back, cautiously to his apartment. After he closed the door to his room, he undressed to his white Jockey briefs. After he sat down at the desk, he wrote a poem at a frantic, compulsive pace, about the seashore with the sand, driftwood, kelp, and the brown and white foam of the incoming waves. He wrote, passionately, describing the erotic dance of the kelp, driftwood, and rocks all intertwined in a sexual act. When he finished writing, arousal had taken over his body. But this event remained suppressed in silence. How could he express how he felt?

A storm of unequaled magnitude raged, one night. The rain pelted the mountain crag outside the living room window. He stared at the stunted, dark, green Coast Live Oak trees and chaparral, growing on the steep slope. The mountainside bubbled with cascading splashes of streams, tumbling over rounded rocks. Fragrant yellow blossoms of wild mustard sent a tingling shivering sensation, rushing through Pablo's blood. This event inspired Pablo's romantic essence of nature's beauty. He would never forget that night. He decided to climb that worn down mountain, during that storm with its blustery winds and drenching rain. He struggled to ascend that peak. Soaked with water, slipping and falling in gorges with the ebbing slides of mud, he finally reached the top of that old volcano. The wind howled, blowing sheets of water into his eyes. He attempted to focus down on his apartment, his friends, and the town of San Luis Obispo. The vengeance of a storm blinded his vision, atop the mountain. With fire in his blood keeping him warm, he tried to keep his sight clear and withstand the ferocity of the storm. His thundering heart throbs warned him of another time in his life when he would have to hold this moment close to him. He had to remember, climbing that mountain with an instinctive purpose to continue living as a part of nature.

At the top of this ancient volcano the wind suddenly calmed, with not a breath of wind blowing. But the rain continued to pelt down on him. All appeared silent. Standing there alone, he saw a light within, the gift of which he had always searched. Remembering a poem he had written, he tried to capture this light close. He envisioned living alone in a cabin in the Trinity Alps, the single glow of light shining from a candle inside a window. In this cabin he wrote his fantasies, only nature, silence, and solitude mattering. As he wrote, he remembered that moment atop the mountain in the storm, his bond with nature keeping him alive to survive, even though there was no one else in his life. When the fury of the wind returned, he wanted to scream out at the night, *I am here and I have something to say*. With only the savage wind echoing down the hillside, he thought. *This event I will remember*.

That Christmas, the roommates inserted a red light bulb into their swag-chained light, hanging from the popcorn ceiling, in the corner front window. They strung twisted strands of white toilet paper to create an illusion of a Christmas tree lit by that single red light bulb. Later that night, they traveled to Dairy Queen for snacks on a study break. Eight young men packed into Sloop's VW bug, one in the trunk, and seven inside. Pablo's friends laughed as they passed Christmas tree lots full of freshly cut green firs and spruces. Pablo bellowed out with the full extent of breath in his lungs, "Murders, butchers, murderers." He did not want people to buy the trees. He insisted on preserving the forests. His roommates seemed amused, but he had taken his out outbursts and convictions very seriously. He began his convictions as a conservation activist that night.

That spring Pablo became more of the person, defining Pablo, marching to a new, different drum, as it did for three of his other roommates. Chester dropped out of school to travel, learn more about people, music, and the spiritual side of life. Russell pined for more intensive studies in art, needing to learn more about painting, sketching, and graphics. Sloop longed to be with his high school sweetheart. Pablo wanted to explore nature and human relationships more than designing buildings. He sought the vision of enlightenment. But most of all, he wanted to express himself through writing. Longing for another man's body, continued to haunt him.

Later in early spring, Mystic Madonna and he climbed the mountain, painted with wild, yellow mustard, blue lupine, and other blooming wild flowers. He knew she and he felt the same way about nature. When they realized they were equal but different as romantics, they bonded in silence as platonic lovers.

He departed his hometown buddies to live outside his dormitory living environment. He began a journey, fending more himself independently in a two bedroom apartment with a straight-laced male, Dan, and his girlfriend, Judy. While the two lovers grappled in their heterosexual, lustful, and sometimes fitful rages of sexual desires in their bedroom, Fat Madonna and Pablo plastered the living room walls with hippie art, such as colorful posters and flyers from the Fillmore Auditorium and the Avalon ballroom. Over the couch they hung an ornate, black and gold, East Indian tapestry, which Pablo purchased in a thrift store in town for three dollars.

His friends and former roommates learned more through the media and word of mouth about a war raging halfway around the world in Viet Nam. It haunted Pablo and them as eligible young men to be drafted and shipped off to a gruesome war without purpose. Their loving companions were equally worried about their fate.

Pablo marched with a very handsome classmate, Spence, against the presence of ROTC on the college campus. Spence was taller with long, dirty blond hair. Pablo and he became very close, so close, that Pablo did not know how to express his romantic feelings. He found himself desiring a man to man, friend-lover relationship. Their bonds became united more by their educational pursuits to understand other cultures through their studies in sociology and anthropology. Pablo wanted to convey an uplifting venture of physical intentions with Spence, but he failed to speak his desires. He thought enlightenment would inspire him. They shared the goal that peace would eventually come. Pablo wanted to scream out to him how he felt, but only silence reigned inside. When spring quarter was coming to a close, they both planned on transferring to the University of California in Santa Barbara for the following fall to study sociology. They knew by fate, they were bound to meet again.

They did meet again at the university in Isle Vista in Spence's beach house apartment. Spence tried to calm Pablo's inner struggles with sexual identity, telling him he had also having the same problem. Pablo had taken LSD and was on a bad trip. His feelings were lost, spinning in racing thoughts of confusion outside the plane of verbal or sexual communication; raging silence prevailed. Spence walked him down to the beach, pleading with him to look at the illuminated plankton in the sand while the waves crashed in. He begged him to look at the stars overhead. He asked him to look for the light, but he saw nothing. Silence had taken command of his being and soul. If only Spence had asked him to scream out to whomever and whatever he listened to in that dark night's ocean setting, Pablo might have been able to express himself. Spence asked him to look at the beautiful ocean, glimmering in the moonlight. Pablo rushed into the water, throwing himself into the crashing waves. Submerged, flailing his arms and legs, he gasped for air, swallowing the briny foam. Spence rushed into the water, wading through the oncoming waves. He picked up Pablo, dragging him back to the beach. He wrapped his arm around Pablo's shoulders, pleading for him to speak, but silence raged within him still.

Decades later, Pablo sat on a deck at the house, deep in a Moraga country canyon at the silent yoga retreat, after a quiet lunch. He looked up to the hillside, cloaked with vividly green oak trees and chaparral, almost hearing the rustling waters of a brook, splashing over and between lichen covered rocks. The hill brought back the vision of that weathered volcano outside the window in the Cal Poly apartment of the Islander the night he climbed the mountain in the ferocious storm. He fondly remembered his fantasies with Spence, with warm desire and their search for truth, light, and peace. He remembered how he thought his yearnings for him, were considered unnatural during those times.

Pablo brushed away what he perceived to be a yellow jacket on his head. His fear of these insects burrowed deep with the memory of his allergic reaction to a single sting. Suddenly, he realized the buzzing around him were not yellow jackets swarming but friendly honey bees, even though he was allergic to those, also. He relaxed, softening his surroundings like Pablo might have done years ago. With the natural scenery encompassing him in warm sunlight, he watched as one bee hummed and hovered around his left foot, crossed over his right leg. He watched it settle down on the white cotton sock. Allowing its wings to cease fluttering, while its fuzzy pollen feeders explored the white cotton, he gazed upon its body with its uniform stripes of brown and yellow. The bee walked slowly, then stopped, and walked, always testing the cloth for nectar. He was not fearful of its potential sting or venom, nor was it frightful of a brushing swing or slap from his hand.

For fifteen minutes they explored and studied each other, with peace in nature's warmth, on a winter's sunlit afternoon. He felt good to be part of this moment, like Pablo in nineteen sixty-seven with the sound, scent, and color of spring on that mountain in San Luis Obispo. The light shone brightly with the bees, his yoga friends, nature, and him.

Pablo awakened from this trance to realize the dawning of another season blossoming in future weeks, with the need for peace still progressing strong, as it did so many years before. It became the process for living as it did for survival; the bee knew, as Pablo did.

Pablo observed the same brilliant, shining light with all his friends at this retreat and with the bees. He originally had reservations of participating in the retreat, since when silence raged, it had been his place of isolation which brought depression and psychosis.

The time arrived for the Buddhist chants and songs with various musical instruments. They sang and made music. They visualized a higher plane of understanding of the universe. They are part of that and pay homage to it, loudly singing with their souls to be heard.

After the musical experience, they went on a meditational walk. The students followed the leader, synchronized by stepping in unison behind each other in silence, walking, together in a steady trance of tranquility through the wooded hillsides and pastures, where horses grazed.

He visualized the light coming from the spirit of doing with others with care, not as a solitary, lonely moment. Times of silence were not a disease or isolation; they were times of peace. Enlightened, silence to him meant a moment to express what was inside; peace, rage, love, sorrow, joy, anger, happiness, ignorance, and knowledge, which was easy for all to express.

When the silent yoga retreat ended he knew Om, Shanti, Om, was the process for, love, joy, light, and knowledge, as the vehicle to peace. Driving home, he glanced at the green chaparral and oak covered hills. The scene reminded him of a time from his past.

Pablo remembered the oil painting hung over the couch in the apartment at Cal Poly, picturing the personality portraits and potential journeys on that ship of life. Russell became an artist of acclaim across the country, also teaching his gift passionately at a university, while Sloop practiced physical therapy and created sculptured garden art at his beach house. Chester traveled worldwide, physically and spiritually, furthering his life in electronics and music, occasionally playing harmonically alongside Ravi Shankar, harmonically, with their sitars singing peace to audiences. Lenny, the sole survivor in completing his degree at Cal Poly in architecture, practiced his career in that subject, traveling around the country and beyond, dabbling in yoga, too.

After Pablo returned home, he wrote, capturing the moments of peace from times of his turmoil.

Months later after the retreat, his partner and he legally joined in marriage, with Anandi performing a spiritual wedding blessing with rose petals, a candle, incense, and a statue of Buddha at their wedding reception, amongst friends and relatives. Another yoga guru, Ramana sang "Time to Say Good Bye" in English and Italian.

Seven years after his marriage, Pablo funneled his fears of silence and its isolation it brought into loving his husband and writing stories and poems, expressing that feeling of peace, he had always sought and would always pursue.

A man-friend-lover relationship continued to blossom with his partner for many years, sharing passionately their physical and spiritual love for each other and the world. Pablo felt one with nature, the light shining within. He would continue to enjoy tranquility with his husband and communing with nature in the garden. He created tales with natural feelings about men loving men to communicate the voice which he knew and continued to hear. The rage of silence continued inside him, at times, but his writing had become the vehicle to express what he must release.

As Pablo looked back at those turbulent times of war and peace during the now forgotten period of the Viet Nam War, he remembered a whole generation who lost their lives and direction. He remembered Spence fondly. Although he searched for him over the years, he was unable to find him to extend his gratitude and those feelings of attraction he desperately needed to express. He understood similar wars were being waged on the other side of the planet in Iraq, Syria, and Afghanistan. He knew the world was divided by cultures, not comprehending the power of peace and releasing their silent rages through non-violent acts. Seven years after his marriage, Pablo funneled his fears of silence and its isolation it brought into loving his husband and writing stories and poems, expressing that feeling of peace, he had always sought and would always pursue. When the silence raged in his heart, he expressed his affection for the man he loved and the solutions to his silence. He knew the silence and rage within was nothing but his passion for life and his party in the universe.

LIMITLESS

by

KL Shandwick

"And those who were seen dancing were thought to be insane by those who could not hear the music."

- Friedrich Nietzsche

I dedicate this to TH

"Don't," she admonished.

"You can't," they chimed in, in unison.

"*Watch me,*" I said.

"Adjust your attitude," he scolded.

"*You adjust yours.*" I shot back at him.

"You must…" the teacher ordered.

"You must not," the powers that be dictated.

"My attitude is fine. I will decide," I replied with confidence.

"Tell me," she demanded.

"It'll never work," he judged.

"Showing, proving it does work is better that telling them."

"Don't do it like that," he reprimanded.

"It would be better if …" she estimated.

"I like it like this," I stated with defiance.

"Who does she think she is?" I overheard.

"What does she think she's doing?" another enquired.

"I know who I am." I smiled.

"*I don't* think *I know what I'm doing.*" I smirked at their impertinent questions.

Worst of all is when they talk about me like I'm not in the room. *Speak to me. Or at least realise I can hear what you are saying.* I wanted to scream at her.

It isn't easy being different in a world where pigeon-holing is the norm.

It's hard being different, while being judged by those who are ordinary.

'The Magic Normal Thinkers Club.'

It doesn't matter to us if we're not members because our club is more elite. It's the way it is. There are less of us. But, consider this; like you, some things are the same. We have emotions and reactions just like everyone else. We may not have the same abilities but if you look hard enough we have much to teach all who are fortunate enough to be normal.

Different can be good. Our thoughts are a rainbow of color, in a world where the stark normality of others can appear in black and white. To us different people anyway. We can co-exist and be valued for our contribution to life because we have a lot to give.

Different means thinking out of the box, doing things another way. It means doing things in a variety of different ways but still attaining the same standard. Often the same task done in different ways obtain the same results. Sometimes even better ones. When it does turn out better—sometimes I've heard them say it must be a fluke. To us, our efforts are the solution to the problem as *we* see it. As the wise words state in that old quotation, "*There's more than one way to skin a cat.*"

Understanding how any mind works– how unique we all are isn't that complex to someone with insight. We don't all look the same. We don't walk the same, or even talk the same. We look at art and we interpret different things in the same picture. That's a difference right there.

We can't always see their reasoning but that fact doesn't seem to matter because there are more of them. Therefore, in their eyes they have to be right.

It takes guts to be different, but I'd rather be like me than someone I'm not. My mind isn't closed and it may not work perfectly, but it's mine. Not theirs—*mine*. So fuck them and their judgements and lectures and poking their nose into what's *mine*. I learn differently from others. That's all. Don't restrict my learning.

So because my thinking is not the same as most I am limitless. Limitless means no boundaries. No mental constraints about how something should look. It's more about how something could look– would look, if only more people thought the way I did. Being limitless means embracing difference, defying difference.

Call it ignorance on my part if you like, but in my view, acceptance is not a bad thing, technically speaking but in my view it means conforming— a mental prison for those of us who don't think the same. I can't conform and still be limitless. I'd rather be limitless than live my life trying to conform to normality. If that means they don't understand me, the problem is theirs– not mine. It takes courage to be proud of being different. We can't all be the same. We are shaped by what life gives us. If I can accept that then I can be at peace with being different. Limitless.

THE FIRST

by

Elizabeth Butts

"Og mens jeg er i live, lad li' et barn mig blive." And while I am alive, let me be as a child.

- Dutch Proverb

I dedicate this story to my beautiful niece.

Joanna somehow felt the alarm clock going off in her sleep before she even heard it. How did things like that happen, anyway?

She reached out from under the bed covers, slapping at air until she finally made contact with the offending piece of machinery. Her small alarm clock hit the wall and she heard the batteries hit the ground alongside the thunk of the clock. Crap, that meant she would have to get up, because there would be no relying on the benevolence of the snooze alarm today.

She groaned as she pushed herself into a seated position. Why was she so groggy? Oh, that's right. Minimal sleep last night. Problem one was a book that refused to be put down for the night. Problem two was today. Today was the worst day. She had to deal with this day every year. It was the first day. But it was a worst first day. It was the first day of her job. Her first day of her first job.

Every year when she started school, she had to stare down the walls, aiming her sight about five feet in front of her on the floor. She would will her hands to hold tight to the books and notebooks she clenched to her chest. Because maybe if she held on tight enough, they wouldn't see. They would never know. Inevitably, she'd slip up. Sometimes it was that first day, sometimes it was after a week. But it would always happen.

Earthquake. That's what they called her. When the tremors started in her fingertips. Her hands would become uncontrollable, taking on a life of their own. She would bite her lip to keep the tears at bay. They could never know how much she despised that name. She would never give them the satisfaction of seeing the wound that their words cut deep into her heart. Her head would hold high, sometimes too high, as she tensed her whole body in an effort to hold still.

Over time, she'd learned to anticipate what would bring on the episodes. Usually stress or excitement. Or embarrassment. Or extreme happiness. Okay, to be honest, sometimes all it took was breathing. She learned to put her hands in her pockets. She would sit on them in class. Anything to look normal, whatever that meant.

But today, today was new. Today was the start of her life. Her real life. Her 'I have a job and am like, totally, an adult' life. She snorted to herself at the thought of being an adult. Today was beyond excitement, which means it might not be controlled. The 'Earthquake' might be let loose with no chance of calming it down. Which made her nervous. She could feel her fingers starting to tap a rhythm all its own on her legs. She grasped her hands together, wringing them together as she tried to deep breathe her way to calm.

Dressing was a unique experience. Initially she had picked out this killer button down top that she'd paired with a pencil skirt that made her legs look about a mile long. However, she had to bail when the buttons were not cooperating. So a short sleeve sweater with a belt won the wardrobe competition. She remembered a therapist once telling her that she should just keep it simple. Yeah, she got it. But she liked cute clothes as much as anyone. Heck, more than anyone!

Makeup was minimal as always. Bronzer, lip gloss and off she went. She knew a lot of people her age would go all drama with their eyes, but she tried mascara once. She swore that off pretty quickly once the stinging in her eye subsided. She would be blind in a week if she attempted that level of war paint!

She looked at herself in the mirror after zipping up her knee high boots and took a hugely deep breath. Exhaling she reminded herself that he earned this. She worked her butt of for this job. She won. There were five final candidates, and she won. She, Joanne. She, Earthquake. Today was the first day.

She walked through the front door of Drexel Associates where she would be starting as an entry level graphic artist. That's right, graphic artist. She smirked as she remembered her art teachers despairing over her inability to draw a straight line. How her attempts at their perfect little art assignments would end up in a bottom drawer. That was the fuel she needed in her fire. She took graphic art classes during the summer and because she could use a computer, and she had found her calling. She was close to failing art in public school; but during the summers she was praised for her genius and creativity.

Standing in the lobby she quickly shook her head to banish the memory of failure out of her mind. Because failure was not what she was about. Ataxia was what she had. It would never, ever define what she could do.

"Hi, I'm Joanna Danielson. I'm the new assistant to the graphic art department. I'm supposed to be meeting Mr. Collins here? It's my first day." Her voice was starting to creep up in pitch as she spoke to the sweet looking older woman behind the desk.

"Yes, Ms. Danielson. I have it right here that you were starting today. Here's your lanyard and credentials that will get you through the building. I will just call Mr. Collins now to let him know you are here."

"No need, Joyce. I saw Joanne coming in. Welcome, Joanne! I hope that the commute wasn't too bad this morning."

"Not bad at all, Mr. Collins. It's good when you're from the area and can take the back roads."

"Great, glad to hear. Call me Bryan. Let's show you your area, and give you the grand tour."

As they walked, the heels of her boots clicked on the porcelain tile flooring they had. She looked around, absorbing the sights in a way she hadn't be able to during the interview process. She was really excited to see where she was working. She couldn't wait to get her hands on the kinds of technology that Drexel Associates would have available to her.

She passed by a door on the way to her new desk and read the placard.

Ashlyn Drexel, Creative Director.

She hadn't had the opportunity to meet Ashlyn in the interview process. She was shocked when she found out that she had been hired to work for the owner's daughter. This only added to her nerves. She avoided looking into the office as she walked by, and seconds later she found herself standing in front of the most beautiful computer she'd ever seen. She leaned back and double checked the name on the cubical half wall. Yup, it said Joanna Danielson. She may have let out a little whimper as she reached out a trembling hand to touch the Apple iMac standing in front of her. She didn't even care that Bryan saw her hand shaking.

He was smiling at her as she looked reverently at her new best friend. He probably thought she was a little crazy, but she didn't care. This was the computer of her dreams.

"I almost don't think you could handle it if I told you that we upgrade every two years."

"Oh my God, you are such a tease!" She slapped a hand over her mouth. Now he would totally think she was flirting with him.

"Um, I'm so sorry, that was totally inappropriate, wasn't it?"

He let out a deep rumbly laugh that made her belly warm a little. A quick glance to the ring finger that was empty surprised her. She must be insane to even think about a guy at work like that! Mental forehead slap.

"You will find out pretty quickly that it takes a lot to be considered 'inappropriate' around here."

Staccato heels clicking on the tile approached quickly.

"Hi, you must be Joanna, I'm so sorry I wasn't able to meet you at the door when you arrived, I got stuck on an early conference call. I'm Ashlyn."

Joanna was shocked to be looking at a woman who was only maybe about five years older than her, dressed almost identically. She gave herself a little high five and pat on the back for the perfect first day outfit.

Suddenly she realized something as she reached to shake her new bosses' hand. It shocked her to the core. It was not expected. It was beyond her wildest expectations. It was perfection.

The gorgeous and perfect Ashlyn Drexel, the owner's daughter, held out a hand that was shaking. It had an uncontrollable tremor and a mind of its own.

She grasped Ashlyn's hand and smiled from ear to ear.

"I can't wait to get started. I've been beyond excited. I honestly had to try about five shirts because I was too excited to be able to button up my first choice!"

Ashlyn laughed and looked relieved.

"I know exactly what you mean. Great choice, by the way. I think this is going to work out perfectly. I am so thrilled you are here and that you chose to come work with us. You were the top candidate because your work was impeccable. No one else's portfolio even came close."

Joanna just let the feeling of happiness and pride roll over her. This was the best first. She was chosen not out of pity. She was chosen not because the owner looked at her and saw someone like his daughter. She was chosen because she was the best. Her heart was pounding with euphoria. Her hands decided to join in the celebration, and for the first time, on the first day of her first job, she was perfect being just Joanna.

BAREFOOT DANCE

by

Audrina Lane

Barefoot Dance

I slip off my shoes
A tentative touch to the floor
The wood beneath them cold
On my toes
It surges up my leg
But I am ready for the beat
To flow through my body
The Rhythm vibrates
Slow at first
Like the drip of a tap
Closing my eyes I swirl, swoop and glide
The tempo increases in twos and fours
The sweat starts to drip, I push on
The pulsing inside me, growing and persistent
I try to keep up, but I may explode
The frenzy, frenetic feet to the beat
The peak is reached
I pause and descend
The music slowly, soothing, trance like
My eyelids close
In deep relaxation, prone, at peace
I feel them cool
My bare feet

DON'T LET ATAXIA DEFINE YOU!

by

Erica Richer

"You must do things you think you cannot do."

- Eleanor Roosevelt

I would like to dedicate this to my daughter Emma, I hope you never let anything hold you back from all the amazing experiences life has to offer. As well as to my friends and family, who've loved and supported me through everything, and always helped me to see the good in even the worst moments!

October 2015,

We limit ourselves more than our illness does!

I have Friedreich's Ataxia BUT I'm much more than that...

I'm also 27, was married this year, bought a house this year, started going back to school this year, have an 18 month old, am 23 weeks pregnant, am an author, have career goals, have family goals, and have plans in life. Don't let a disorder keep you from making your life extraordinary!

Having Ataxia doesn't have to define you! So the question is who are you?

THE BEAUTIFUL EXPERIMENT

by

K D Grace

"Beauty is truth, truth beauty,—that is all

Ye know on earth, and all ye need to know"

- John Keats

Dedicated to all of the fascinating, truly beautiful people in the world. Their story is truth, and in that truth, beauty.

I was bored. My flight had been delayed. I'd already been traveling forever, and I'd reached that point at which I was too tired to read, too tired to concentrate on writing, too tired to sit still without being twitchy. I didn't want to drink, I didn't want to eat. I just wanted to be done travelling. That's when I began The Beautiful Experiment. I was seated off one of the main concourses, which was a constant hive of activity -- people coming and going, popping in and out of shops and scurrying to make tight connections. It was the ideal place to people watch -- but with a twist. I decided to watch the masses to see just how many truly beautiful people I could spot.

Okay, I know everyone has a slightly different ideal when it comes to beauty, but we all know it when we see it. We all know that look that turns heads, that look that makes us want to stare, to take in all that loveliness just a little longer. I didn't care if the real lookers were men or women. I mean if we're honest, we look at both, whether we admire their beauty, want it or envy it. So I sat and I watched. … and I watched … and I watched. Since that time I've carried out my little experiment in pubs, in museums, on the tube in London, in busy parks, and the results are always the same. There just aren't that many real stunners out there!

I was struck by that fact in the airport, so I decided to add another dimension to my experiment. I decided to look for people who were interesting. It didn't necessarily have to be their looks that were interesting; it could just as easily be their behaviour, their dress, something, anything that made them worth a surreptitious stare. And wow! Being delayed in an airport suddenly became a fascinating gristmill for story ideas and intriguing speculation.

I've carried out this experiment lots of time now, and the results are always the same. There are very few stunners out there, and even when I spot one, even when I find myself sneaking glances at a beautiful person, my eyes, and my attention, can always be drawn away by the interesting people.

In erotica and, in particular erotic romance, the characters are usually voluptuous, sculpted beauties and broad shouldered, washboarded hunks. It's fantasy after all. But how long can a story focus the reader's attention on washboard abs or perfect tits? Descriptions give us a handle. Descriptions are like the label on a file. They might attract us to the file, but if the file is empty, it won't hold our attention. It's what makes the described beautiful person interesting that makes the story, it's their scars – both inside and out – and how they deal with those scars, that make them more than just a billboard for perfume or designer underwear.

In our genre, sex is a large part of what makes our beautiful people intriguing; how they think about sex, their kinks, their quirks, their neuroses, their baggage – all of those things make the fact that our beautiful people are interesting way more important than the fact that they're beautiful. Add to that some seriously delicious consequences for that sex, some chaos and mayhem, a few character flaws that catch us off our guard, that draw us in and voila! A gripping story is born!

Perfection in a story, in characters, is the equivalent of a literary air brushing. No flaws = no story; no rough spots = nothing to hold our attention. Our characters' beauty is only their handle. Their flaws and their intriguing quirks, what lies beneath that beauty are what catapult us into the plot, what make us want to stay on for more than just a look-see and to dig a little deeper, to really know those characters and become emotionally involved with them.

I am reminded again and again as I grow older that so much of what we view as beauty these days is youth, and we all have that, but only for a short time. That's the blank slate before life roughs us up a bit and time does its frightful magic on us, the one that gives us wisdom, knowledge, experience, makes us interesting, but at the price of our youth.

Last night on the tube in London, I tried my little experiment again, just to make sure. More data is always a good idea, and good science has to be repeatable, doesn't it? Taking into account my own preferences and prejudices, the results were the same. I can remember a half a dozen really interesting people, people I could easily write a story about. There wasn't a single stunner among them, which leads me to the conclusion that we're more interesting in our flaws than in our perfections. We're more interesting in our experiences and the way they manifest than in the static youth and beauty of the moment. It also excites me to think that I'm surrounded by interesting people all the time. A story is never farther away than the next intriguing person. Is this an ordinary-looking person's version of sour grapes? I don't think so; I hope not. Truth is there's an astonishing transformation that takes place in the company of truly interesting people. Before long, right before my eyes, those truly intriguing people become the beautiful people. There's always a story in that.

BATTERED WITH LOVE STRIPES

by

Kim Black

"You are too beautiful to be belittled,

Too brave to be beaten

And too blessed to be broken!"

- Pastor Marcus Gill,

Founder and Lead Pastor of the Rush Church United

To those who thought they were destined to repeat the mistakes of their parents...

Know that you aren't.

Know that you can break the cycle.

Know that there is freedom and peace in the Lord.

The Past

WHEN I WAS a little girl I told myself that I wouldn't end up like my mother. I loved her, truly and deeply, but I didn't want to be anything like her.

She was a strong woman in so many ways, but when she broke down, she really broke down. I can still recall the screaming that rang out through my childhood home. The fights that seemed to stretch on and on through the night—the fear my brother and I felt coursing through us minute by minute, hour by hour and even for days on end.

The word "traumatic" doesn't even begin to cover what my childhood was like. We lived in constant fear, praying for a divorce that just never came.

Was it crazy that divorce was what my brother and I most wished for? Sad perhaps? Messed up? Definitely. But, that was what we hoped for, especially on those long, scary nights.

Most people don't know this, but I hate Thanksgiving. It sounds crazy to say that out loud, but it's the truth. I hate that holiday and everything about it.

That wasn't always the case, of course. It used to be one of my favorite holidays. We'd always throw a party and invite all of our family over for Thanksgiving dinner. We were a partying bunch, always quick to throw a big bash and Thanksgiving was a huge affair every year.

I can't remember how old I was one particular Thanksgiving— the one year that affected me so deeply that I would forever dislike the holiday, but it's hard to forget what was the worst day of my life.

I was in junior high school at the time, probably eleven or twelve years old, but I remember everything about that day as if it had all happened only yesterday.

The party was a success. All our family members had full bellies, and the music that had been playing on the stereo was turned off as everyone started to leave.

It was probably about 2:00 a.m. I say that because there wasn't much on T.V. and my brother and I had just parked ourselves in our parent's bedroom, surfing through the channels until we landed on the Cartoon Network.

It was barely five minutes later when we heard the screaming coming from the living room. Scared and in a panic, my brother and I got up and ran there at full speed. When we finally reached my parents, I could hear my heart beating loudly in my ears. My skin flushed as I took in the scene before me.

A scream erupted from my mother's mouth as my father yanked her by her hair and proceeded to bash her head against every nearby surface and wall.

I don't remember how we got him off of her, but we somehow managed to do just that. My brother, my mother and I actually made it into our bedroom just as my father pushed our bedroom door open to where we cowered inside. The butter knife in his hand worried me and I cannot remember ever hating him more than I did that night.

He tried to get us to leave him and my mother alone in the room, my room, but, of course, we refused to leave. It was an hour later that he finally walked out of our room, but we were unable to rest that night, in fact, we couldn't really rest any night after that. Who knew when he would lose it again?

So, no, I didn't want to be like my mom. I didn't want to be married to man I could never trust. I didn't want to be tied to such a man, knowing that he didn't have any reservations about hurting me.

"I will never allow any man to pound on my face," I always said to myself.

Have you ever heard that old adage, "Never say never"? I didn't fully understand the meaning of that saying until I was much older.

The Decision

HIS NAME WAS Donald Smith and he was twenty-six years old, which made him approximately eleven years older than me, but most of the time neither of us remembered the age difference. People always said that I had an old soul, but Donald always seemed to be younger than I was.

He was a singer that I met through Sharon, the girl who was my best friend at the time. Sharon was twenty-five years old, and she allowed me to live with her after I left my parent's house, which was about the time I turned fifteen. I know exactly what you're thinking, "What is a fifteen-year-old doing living with a friend instead of with her parents?" Well, I hope you're sitting down, because it's a long story.

Really!

It all started when my ex-boyfriend got locked up. He was involved in a murder. Wait... It's really not what you think. He's not a bad person, he just got caught up some, weird situation and did something stupid. While trying to protect someone, he ended up stabbing the person attacking them, and a month later the person he stabbed died. As a result of his stab wound causing the fatality, he was tried, found guilty and sent to prison, leaving me alone and kind of lost. After all the sobbing and sleepless nights, I decided to better my life for him. I wanted to become successful for him. I wanted to make him proud by becoming a lawyer. When it came time for him to get out, I would have a house set up and ready for him, but that plan fell through after I received one phone call.

The telephone call was from John, who was a close friend of mine. He called to wish me a happy birthday. I didn't realize at the time that my life was about to completely change, but it did. He told me that my ex-boyfriend had cheated on me and had impregnated the other woman before he was arrested and jailed.

I was both crushed and hurt and I had no idea how to cope with his betrayal. It was then that I started to throw away all that was important in my life, including God.

It all started with the move.

The Move

I MET SHARON through some friends at school. I had just run away from home, without a thought or plan in mind as to how I would manage to survive on my own. Sharon had a two-bedroom apartment she shared with her sister, although her sister didn't really spend much time at all in the apartment.

It was really a mess of a place, but I just wanted to have a place where I could hang out with my friends and have a good time. It was on my first night there that I had my first taste of alcohol and my first toke of marijuana. Why I even tried it seems crazy to me now. I wasn't the type of person you'd think might be easily coaxed into doing something illegal, but my tough exterior affect was all bullshit. I wanted to fit in with this crowd, even if it was only for that one night. So, when they passed the joint my way, I took a toke, and then took several more tokes throughout the night.

By morning, I had a huge headache and not a clue as to where I was. It took me a few minutes to get my bearings, but Sharon had gone out and left me there all alone.

With nothing else to do, I proceeded to do what I did best. I cleaned. I cleaned everything. By the time I was done, you could eat off of the floor.

I started to worry that when Sharon returned, she might think that what I'd done was a bit rude, as if I was suggesting that she didn't know how to clean her own house, although it was quite apparent she really didn't, but that's beside the point. I simply didn't want her to get upset with me.

To my surprise and relief, she wasn't offended at all. She loved what I had done to clean her apartment and she told me that I could continue to stay with her if that was what I wanted to do. I more than wanted to, I needed to stay with her, since I had no intention of going back home anyway.

My relationship with Sharon went well. I'd help out wherever and whenever I could and she allowed me to stay with her. I met her friends and family. Her sister was a wary woman, but she was nice enough, and her brother, Donald, lived in New Jersey.

Sharon told me a little bit about her brother before I actually met him. She told me that they resembled one another, and that he had experienced some difficulty with women. 'Difficulty' was not quite the correct word to use when describing Donald's relationship issues.

Donald was an abuser and everyone seemed know it. What made it even worse was that I knew it, but did I take fact that into consideration? Nope. I had to learn this the hard way and boy, did I ever learn.

I'm not sure what made me even consider a relationship with Donald. But from the first day Sharon introduced us, he claimed me. Maybe it was because he was so much older than I was. Maybe, in my mind, I thought that I was above being abused and that even if I dated him it just would never happen. Or, maybe somewhere in my fifteen-year-old mind, I thought it would be okay. I really can't tell you why I didn't think twice about dating him. But that's what I did. From the first day we met, I was his.

Oddly enough, I just never even considered he would ever hit me. I know it makes no sense looking back on it now. It was actually really stupid on my part. All I can say is that at fifteen, I had no business being in that relationship at all. But at the time... I thought he was the moon, the stars... you get the idea.

You'd better sit down for this one.

Donald and I were together for almost nine months and things between us were going well. We became close and found that we had a lot in common, especially when it came to music. We spent many long nights staying up and just talking about music. Those talks were really what kept us together. He loved the fact that I had the same passion for music as he did. He would sometimes smile at me and tell me that he was starting to fall in love with me.

One night I went out with my best friend, John, and his buddies. We had a lot to drink and I was feeling a bit buzzed and dizzy as I headed home.

I got home at about one o'clock in the morning and I was exhausted. Sharon had also gone out that night and had taken the keys to the apartment with her. Donald was home, but I didn't want to wake him. I tried calling Sharon, but she wasn't answering her phone, and so I was left with no choice but to call Donald.

The phone rang and rang but he didn't pick up the call. He wasn't a deep sleeper, so I was certain that he'd be able to hear the phone ring. I waited downstairs for about a half-hour when I decided to pick up the phone and try calling him again.

After about four rings, Donald finally answered in a strange tone of voice and told me he was coming to open the door.

If I had known what was about to happen to me, I would have just slept on the steps outside until Sharon came home and let me inside. But no, I went upstairs and for the next three hours I learned how it felt to stand in my mother's shoes.

The Victim

DONALD STARTED WITH just a couple of smacks across my face. I don't know where the first one came from, but it really shook me up. He asked me to explain where I'd been, but before I could fully answer his question, he hit me again, only this time it was harder and with his closed fist. I tried to block some of his punches, but I couldn't.

I didn't know what to do or say to get him to stop hitting me. I tried to back away from him, but that only angered him more. He was like an enraged animal.

When his hands got tired of hitting me, he grabbed an umbrella. You know which kind, the tall, long ones. I saw him pick it up and I started to freak out. It had a wooden handle that broke when it hit my small 105-pound body.

I will never forget the sound that echoed through the living room as he swung that thick umbrella at me, and landed the blow against my back. I slumped over, nearly falling to the floor. Just thinking about it now brings back the terrible pain I felt then.

If he had stopped at the umbrella I would have been all right, but that was just the beginning. Oh no, there was more to come, and the next thing he used on me was his belt with its thick metal buckle. Each time he hit me with it, it hurt so badly that I wished for death. At least then I wouldn't have to deal with the physical pain.

I tried to calm him down, and I kept asking him why he was doing this to me. "Me Donald, me? Not me!! I only care for you, and I take care of you. I've never tried to hurt you, so why are you hitting me?" I couldn't believe what was happening and as the minutes turned into hours, I began to hate him for what he was doing. I despised him and I no longer wished for my death, but his.

The first hour went by and still he continued to torture and hurt me. When the belt buckle broke, he started using again his hands on me again. Those strong, heavily veined hands, oh his came at me quickly and repeatedly.

This was the man that once claimed to love me. This man, whom I once thought would never hurt me like he had the others was doing just that. This couldn't be happening to me!

I remembered running inside Sharon's kid's bedroom where I woke them up by yelling, "Help me, please, help!" The twin boys were just five years old, how could they possibly have helped me? I instantly regretted running into their room. The looks on their faces mirrored the look that I remembered on my own face when my father was beating my mother.

My face swelled to the size of a basketball. My lip was split and I no longer had my milk chocolate complexion. I was darker now, covered with deep purple bruises. "Stop please," I begged him, "can't we talk about this?"

This time he dragged me into the little closet-sized bathroom which gave me no room to back away from him or run away and try to escape him.

He continued to yell and scream at me, accusing me of cheating on him with John. I told him time and time again that John and I were just friends. I tried to explain, but he just wasn't hearing it, and each time I opened my mouth, he made me eat his fist.

He beat me for three hours, tormenting me, yelling at me, telling me that I was cheating when I wasn't. I cried and cried and still he was utterly heartless. It was no wonder his friends gave him that word as his nickname. He didn't have a heart at all, and with every punch, smack and lick he landed, he stripped down my heart, leaving it every bit as cold and void as his own.

He wanted me to admit to cheating on him, but how could I admit to something I hadn't done? How could I say I was with someone I hadn't been with? I simply couldn't do that and he couldn't be reasoned with—he just didn't understand. When he finally realized that he was getting nowhere, he left the bathroom to go and get his knife.

I knew that he was getting his knife because Donald had a reputation for having stabbed girlfriends in the past, and from the looks of it, I was going to be his next target. I was about to become another victim to add to the list of his previous victims, or possibly my name might appear in tomorrow's newspaper obituary column.

I couldn't just stand there and allow this to happen. I asked God for the whys and hows in my head and I knew that I couldn't just to nothing and allow him to kill me, so I ran out of the bathroom and raced to the door.

I got to the stairs and quickly ran down several flights of them. I was determined to escape this vicious and crazed man. I hoped I'd run into someone who would help me, and that I did.

The Restoration

I RAN STRAIGHT into God's arms. He was glad He could help. What's funny is that you will never believe where I ran into God. It was in the incinerator room on the third floor of the apartment building. "Thank you, thank you, thank you, Jesus! Oh God," I whispered to myself softly, while hiding in that little room.

Donald ran after me, but he didn't realize that I had ducked inside the incinerator room. It was my safe haven from Donald.

I stayed there for about an hour and a half. I prayed that Donald wasn't still walking around looking for me or waiting for me to come out so he could continue beating me.

My heart was pounding so quickly as I slowly opened the door and peeked outside. Seeing no one, I ran to a random apartment door and rang the doorbell, but no one answered. It was then that I heard pots and pans clanging together.

I rang the bell once again and a lady finally came to the door. She was a heaven-sent angel. She took care of me that night, telling me that she had gone through the same thing herself. She was a Christian and was very sweet.

Later that night, I went to the bathroom and slowly made my way to the toilet seat. I pulled off my pants and took a good look at my legs. My legs, my sides, my arms, and every part of me was badly bruised. I thought I had hit the ultimate low, but that was before I stood up, looked in the mirror, and saw what was left of me.

I stared into my empty soulless eyes. The image looking back at me was not the person that I knew. It was someone else. I was no longer the happy Christian girl I used to be. I was empty inside and God had allowed all of what had happened to me to occur so that I could reach this very moment of self-realization. As I stared into the mirror, my basketball-sized head, my black and blue eyes, and my busted lip, I finally saw them as love stripes from God.

Most people wouldn't get it. They wouldn't understand how or why I would say that what had happened to me that night was that I'd received love stripes from God. But that's what it was, and that's how I saw it.

Before I left my parent's home and threw everything away, I was serving Him—following Him, and, because I couldn't deal with what my ex-boyfriend had done to me, I had unknowingly turned my back on God. The safety and the comfort He had always shown me was gone and I had allowed my fears to become my reality.

Thankfully, He would never give me more than I could bear. He knew that I would come to understand how I'd ended up in this situation. He knew that I would see it for what it was. It was a wake-up call, because I didn't belong in a world where I was high and drunk most days, a world in which I was in a very unhealthy relationship with a man eleven years my senior. I didn't belong there. I belonged with Him.

Sometimes things happen to us and we are quick to blame the devil or blame other people. I have often done this in my life, but then I remember that some things happen to us for a reason, to push us out of horrible situations and to rise above them. Sometimes bad things happen to save us, and this was my bad thing and it was the push I needed.

Without what had happened to me that night, who knows where I would have ended up? Who knows if I would still be alive? Now I can say, with certainty, that I know from personal experience what my mother went through. I am not like her when it comes to bad relationships. I can choose to leave. But, in one way, I am just like her because I believe in a God that will always have my back and who will always send me a means of escape when I most need it. That's all she ever wanted for me.

That incinerator saved my life, and His angel comforted me in my time of need.

HOPE

by

C.A.Bell

"Don't cry because it's over, smile because it happened."

- Dr. Seuss

"Inspiration comes from within yourself. One has to be positive.
When you're positive, good things happen."

- Deep Roy

Dedicated to my daughter, Emm

Hope

I lost something one day,
A piece of me was destroyed.
My mind wouldn't compute anymore,
My heart was now a void.
I lost something one day,
A light that shone so bright.
Something that I yearned for,
And planned to hold so tight.
I lost someone one day,
My baby one day was taken.
Without warning she was gone,
My heart never to awaken.
I lost my daughter one day,
A day that we never let pass.
We let our Chinese lanterns fly,
And prey their lights will last.
Through all the pain and selfish thoughts,
One man would help me through.
No, not almighty God above,
This man was someone I knew.
The man that I swore to love and obey,
His was the hand that showed me the way.
Without this man there would be no me,
And today we wouldn't have our family.
We have never replaced, nor filled the space,
Just added our love to the human race.
Hoping that pieces of her are passed on,
In the twinkling of eyes, and the smile of our son.

Everyone has been through, going through, or will go through heart
ache. Whether that be the loss of someone dear, divorce, or illness.
And although at times you may feel like your world is at an end,
there is always something or someone out there to help you through.

When times are unbearable and you feel like giving up, remember that you are here for a reason. And if you aren't sure of that reason, you will find it one day. My reason is my family.

There was once a time when I felt guilty to smile or laugh. There was once a time when I felt like my heart would never heal from my loss, and although I still hurt, it's an ache in my heart that I have learned to accepted.

We are all human and built to survive and cope with whatever this world throws our way. Just remember you are here for a reason, if only to be a memory of someone who loves you.

'Thank you to my husband, father, and sister. Without you three I would not have got through, so thank you with all my heart."

TO MA

by

Cathy Schisel Knuth

"Go confidently in the direction of your dreams; live the life you
have imagined."

- Henry David Thoreau

Dedicated to Melissa Ann

To MA

Your hands won't move the way you like
Your legs and feet won't take flight
Your mind is willing to make the moves
But your body won't obey its rules
I promise I won't laugh if you should fall
I will provide you with my hand at your call
I see you as someone whole
 Even as your body is taking the toll
I will be a friend in the depths of my soul

DEPRESSION

by

AT King

Our Greatest Fear

Our deepest fear is not that we are inadequate.

Our deepest fear is that we are powerful beyond measure.

It is our light not our darkness that most frightens us.

We ask ourselves, who am I to be brilliant, gorgeous,

talented and fabulous?

Actually, who are you not to be?

You are a child of God.

Your playing small does not serve the world.

There's nothing enlightened about shrinking so that other

people won't feel insecure around you.

We were born to make manifest the glory of

God that is within us.

It's not just in some of us; it's in everyone.

And as we let our own light shine,

we unconsciously give other people
permission to do the same.

As we are liberated from our own fear,

Our presence automatically liberates others.

- Marianne Williamson

This one is dedicated to everyone who has gone or is going through depression. Keep fighting, it might be difficult now, but it will get better.

Back in mid to late 2007 I came to the realization that my marriage of almost eight years was coming to an end. I had been with my wife at the time for about ten or eleven years total and had never thought that I would be filing for divorce. I kept a smile on my face throughout the whole process and whenever I was around my friends and family, I was always in good spirits and laughing. The problem was, when everyone would leave and I was left alone, I didn't feel like doing anything. I refused to eat or interact with anyone on social media. If my phone would ring I would simply stare at it and contemplate answering it, most of the time I would silence it. My television would be on, but I wasn't aware of the program or movie playing on it. The more people would ask me if I was ok or if I needed anything, the more I wanted to hide away and ask them to leave me alone. I was fine no matter what anyone said. I even got the point where every thought I had going through my head would consist of me either disappearing or killing myself. I believed that my family, friends, and the world would be better without me around. I saw myself as a burden to everyone I came across. I never would have thought that there was something wrong with me. To me, these thoughts were normal. It wasn't until later on that I realized they weren't normal everyday thoughts and that I was suffering from a silent disease; depression.

It is estimated that over 350 million people suffer from this disease. It is something that strikes men and women of all races and ages. Many people refuse to admit they suffer from it—I know I did at first—and many see it as a weakness. Even worse is that some people don't even know they are going through it because they aren't aware of what it is. I decided to google the definition of depression and here is what I found;

de·pres·sion

də ˈpreSH(ə)n/

noun

noun: depression; plural noun: depressions

1. feelings of severe despondency and dejection.

"Self-doubt creeps in and that swiftly turns to depression"

PSYCHIATRY

a mental condition characterized by feelings of severe despondency and dejection, typically also with feelings of inadequacy and guilt, often accompanied by lack of energy and disturbance of appetite and sleep.

In my own words and experience, depression is a series of feelings and thoughts that slowly creep into your mind and break you down. Depression causes the one suffering from it to slowly detach themselves from their family and friends and sink into a dark place within. In this place, you only think of what is going wrong and of all the negative things in your life. You cannot be bothered with such tasks as eating or being active in your community. The mere thought of dragging yourself out of bed and dealing with people is enough to send you into a dark corner of the room, where you can sit quietly for hours or even days, hoping that no one comes looking for you.

Depression can be caused by many different things. Some people get hit because of an incident that happened at home, or because they aren't doing well at work or school. Being bullied or in an abusive relationship can also cause depression to set in. Getting bad news from a doctor, like learning you have cancer, aids, or some other illness, can certainly cause depression to set in over time. In some cases, depression has been experienced by women who just gave birth or parents who just had children leave the house because they have gone off to college or gotten married. For me, it was the fact that I was going through a divorce, something I never expected to deal with.

As I said before, many people go through this and some don't even realize they are going through it until it is too late. There is help out there but not everyone seeks it or is even aware that it is available. They spend their time thinking of how they are not good enough to be helped or don't deserve the help, and because of that, some will succumb to it and cause themselves harm, which may lead to death. It is a very debilitating disease if it goes unnoticed, untreated, or is allowed to take hold of someone for a long period of time. It is difficult to catch and easy to hide. It can be written off or dismissed by simply saying "it's just a phase, I'll get over it soon just leave me alone to deal with it", but that is a lie we tell ourselves. It is not a phase, and nobody, I don't care who you are, can get over it on their own. These are the six things that helped me get through my dark and desolate time and I am simply sending this out there in hopes that it helps someone who is going through it or that it gives you the insight so that you can better prepare yourself to help someone fight through it. I will list what helped me and later go into explaining them and try to give an example and shed some light on it.

1. ADMITTING THE PROBLEM EXISTS

2. ASK FOR HELP

3. ACCEPT THE HELP

4. FIND A HOBBY

5. TAKE THINGS 1 DAY AT A TIME

6. REALIZE THAT IT IS A PART OF YOU

ADMITTING THE PROBLEM EXISTS

I know this sounds like an easy thing to do, but believe me, it is more difficult than you are aware of. Many of us that suffer from depression are afraid to say it out loud that we are going through it. Why? It could be because of how we've been exposed to it in the movies and television. Usually when someone is depicted of being depressed, they show the extreme side of it. These people are in mental hospitals and are lashing out at everyone trying to help them. They continuously try to hurt themselves and will be shown as outcasts and people who are avoided at all costs. Some of them are sitting in a chair staring out a window with no sign of life or of being aware of where they are, much less what is happening around them, because of all the medication they are on. These people are alone in the world and the only ones who interact with them are the nurses and doctors. Most of us are afraid of being left alone so therefore refuse to acknowledge the fact that we are feeling depressed.

The biggest lie we tell ourselves and our loved ones is that it is just a phase. We say this to keep people from getting too close or prying into our private lives and affairs, I know that is why I had said it. Another common lie I told was that I was ok. When someone would ask how I was holding up, I'd simply put a smile on my face and say that I was doing well and proceed to laugh and have fun. Nobody knew that it was just a façade. On the outside I was fine but on the inside, I was itching and waiting for the time to come for me to get away from everyone. To be able to get back to the quiet confines of my own home and the serene and quiet setting of my bedroom. I knew that once I crawled into my bed, all would be well and I'd feel content, or so I believed.

For months I went on with these games; showing one face to my family and friends except a different person was looking back at me when I'd look in the mirror. To me, this was normal, I believed that everyone lived this way and there was nothing wrong with it. Not once did the thought that there was something wrong every cross my mind. I had heard of people being depressed but I didn't believe that it would ever affect me. I thought I would be immune to it since I had my family and caring friends around me all the time. I was dealing with things my own way so I figured as long as I wasn't hurting anyone, then there was no way I could be depressed.

All I knew was that my marriage was coming to an end and I was starting to lose weight and have many sleepless nights. Everyone always joked that I was losing weight because I was happy, so I went along with it. As for the losing sleep part, I worked in retail and I blamed it on the long hours and rotating shifts that I had to endure throughout the months. I had an excuse for everything that was happening in my life and kept repeating them to myself, as if I was trying to convince myself that it was the truth. Looking back on it I can honestly say that is what I was doing. I don't remember the exact time or date that I finally came face to face with the truth, but I know that it hit me. I remember lying in bed in the middle of the day staring up at my ceiling. It was my day off from work and I had plenty of things that needed to be done, but for some reason, my body refused to move. I thought that I was just overworked and my body needed the rest. I closed my eyes and didn't wake up until several hours later, and that's when I realized I had a problem. It was at that very moment that I dragged myself out of the bed, forced myself to go into the bathroom, and wash my face to wake up completely. Once I had done, that I stared at my reflection and admitted that I needed help. I didn't care who knew it anymore, all I cared about was getting back to being me and not feeling ashamed or afraid of letting anyone know that I believed there was something wrong. I wanted to get better and I didn't care how it happened.

ASK FOR HELP

So here I was in my bathroom with water dripping down my face and I had admitted to myself that I was facing a problem which I had been hiding from my family, friends, and myself. I knew that it would take time to get back to the place I used to be and that there was no way I would be able to get there on my own. If I really wanted to get back to where I used to be, then I was going to have to ask for some help. I had heard stories of people keeping it to themselves and getting hurt and I vowed that would not be me. I refused to hurt myself or anyone else around me because I was too proud to ask for help.

Finding help sounds like an easy thing to do, but with so many choices, someone can be easily overwhelmed. Depending on how hard depression has hit you or a loved one, the choices available can vary. The first and most obvious choice would be your family and/or your friends. If those venues are not a viable option, or if you need a little more help than that, then a support group is another area that can be explored.

Any person dealing with depression can always seek professional help; the most important thing is being able to find someone you are comfortable with. That was my next step. I had my siblings, parents, a friend, or even a doctor. I knew that the person I chose to talk to had to be someone I wouldn't have a problem opening up to. I weighed all my options and found the one person I felt would be the best to help me get through my depression. Although this option worked for me, I can't say that it will be what works for everyone. The level of depression is different in each person; some people might need to seek professional help in order move forward with their lives. Just remember that admitting you have a problem and asking for help is NOT a sign of weakness, but rather a sign that you want to get better.

ACCEPT THE HELP

So now we have admitted that we have a problem and have even asked for help from someone, what's the next step? Believe it or not, the next step is to actually accept the help that is offered. Many people have problems with this and therefore this can be one of the most crucial moments of the whole process. Accepting the help might be more difficult for some people than asking for the help in the first place.

I know what you are thinking and I bet I know the question rolling around in your head…Why ask for help if you aren't going to accept it? The answer is simple, people will ask for help if they see it as a way of getting everyone to leave them alone. Maybe they were pushed into admitting they have a problem and they are still in denial. If you feel someone you know might be suffering from depression, it's not a good idea to push, or bully, them into admitting they are suffering from it. Remember that different people have different attitudes, and just because someone seems depressed, it doesn't mean they are. They could be going through a change and just exploring a different way of self-expression.

Another thing stopping someone from accepting help is pride. Pride can be a good thing, but too much pride can be dangerous. When someone is too proud, they fail to see that they need help and believe they can face anything on their own. If you do get someone who is proud to accept help, they will often try to face the problem on their own, just to prove that they don't need anyone's help. People filled with pride will often see themselves as indestructible, which can be the reason for them to get into deeper problems.

If you are suffering from depression, please be ready and willing to put your pride on the shelf and accept the help that is being offered. I know that it might be a difficult task to do, but in the end, it is the only way to get better and the best way to move forward.

When I realized I needed help, I was worried about how my family and friends would see me once they knew what I was going through and that they'd label me as weak. I even thought that they would never let me forget about it. To my surprise, accepting the help was the best thing I ever did. Not only did it prove me wrong but it brought me closer to my family. They were more than willing to help me get through the dark and difficult times and they didn't make a big deal about it. They made me realize that I wasn't weak by asking them for help, but rather that it was a sign of strength to them. It takes more courage to ask for and accept help than it does to fight through every single battle on your own.

FIND A HOBBY

We are now halfway through the dark times. Let's keep moving and continue to get better. This next step is the one I found to be fun and very flexible; find a hobby. It can be something you are good at or something you have always wanted to do.

There are many things that can be done to pass the time and keep your mind focused and busy. Some of these things take little to no money and can be done by anyone, while others will incur some money to be spent. You can take up photography, go bike riding, draw, make jewelry, or maybe even write. If you aren't sure of what you can do, feel free to go online and look for ideas. Pinterest is a good place to search for great, easy, and inexpensive crafting ideas you can do on your own. Plus you can find things to do for every season throughout the year.

If you want to get out of the house look around your local area and find any nature parks to visit. Most of the parks charge a small fee, but it is affordable and it provides you with a place to lose yourself for hours. If you have a camera at your disposal or can afford to buy one then this is a great place to start your photography venture. Go around and take pictures of the different animals that are native to your area. If you don't feel like going to a nature park, or simply don't have one close by, you can always improvise. I like to go outside during the day and take pictures of the sky using the camera on my phone. During a storm I will go and take some pictures of the dark clouds as they roll in and, if possible, I will also take videos of the storm when it is in full force, especially if there is lightning.

Another hobby I picked up while dealing with my depression was writing. I found that when you can't talk to someone, the next best thing to do is to write it down. Whatever it is you are feeling, whether it be anger, sadness, sorrow, or joy, simply write it down. You don't have it to show it to anyone, it is just a way for you to get your emotions out and hopefully help relieve some of the stress of holding it in. You can keep a log or diary and keep it with you, whenever you get the urge to write something, do it. If you don't like the idea of carrying the journal with you everywhere you go there are other options. Almost every cell phone comes with an app you can use to jot down notes. If it doesn't have one simply download a free one. Use your phone as your own personal journal that you carry everywhere. When I started writing I would always carry a small notepad and a pen with me. After a while I stopped doing that and started using my phone. As soon as I would get home I'd transfer my words to my computer then save the document in a usb flash drive, which I kept with me at all times. I wrote poems for a while but eventually my poetry led me to try writing short stories and that led me to writing books. As of now, I still write poetry to deal with my emotions every once in a while, but my main focus is on my stories.

Just keep in mind that whatever hobby you decide to take up you will enjoy doing it. You don't have to share your works with anyone if you decide to write, it is mainly to help you deal with your emotions and nothing else. Whether you let others read your words is completely up to you. You never know what could come of your hobby; you might find that one hidden talent you never knew was there. Or find a group of people who share your interest and make new friends who can become your support system throughout your ordeal. Don't be afraid to venture out of your comfort zone either, it might just be what you need.

TAKE THINGS ONE DAY AT A TIME

I know it sounds like a cliché, but it truly is the best way to do it. A lot of people think that you will wake up one day and magically feel better, sadly that isn't how it works. You will have some great days and you will have some lousy ones; you must be aware that it is going to happen at some point. You could be having the greatest day and just one little thing will trigger a memory. You slowly feel sadness creep in and you feel the need to get away from everyone and be alone. This is normal; trust me I have been through those days. It is ok to have your moods switch at a heartbeat without rhyme or reason and without warning.

For those who are reading this in hopes of finding a way to help a friend or loved one, there are some things those suffering from depression cannot handle hearing; "Stop feeling that way." "Just smile and get over it.". "What do you have to be depressed about?" I have been told that before several times and it always makes me feel worse, not better.Try and compare it to spraining your ankle or breaking your toe when you stub it on the corner of the bed. We've done them and know they hurt like heck; imagine you were told to stop feeling the pain and just get over it. You wouldn't be able to do it because you can't control the amount of pain you feel. Same with depression, when it hits it can't be controlled; when they have mood swings or depressive episodes, the best thing you can do is to let them deal with it and tell them you are there and available for them if they need someone to talk to. Don't say it because you think it is what they need to hear, say it because you really mean it and want to help them. Understand that they might not want to talk about it right then and there, so don't push them. When they feel ready and willing they will talk to you. More importantly, they will appreciate the fact that you let them to decide on their own when it was right to talk about whatever is bothering them.

For those of you who are going through it, please understand that while I have been through it myself and I know exactly how you feel, pushing those closest to you away isn't the answer. I am simply saying that it is ok to take some time for yourself if you need to. Remember what I said before; if you ask for the help please be willing to take the help that is being offered. I understand that sometimes you just want to be left alone to try to make sense of things and that there are certain memories that you will want to deal with alone, that is perfectly fine. To this day, there are some things that I will deal with internally because I don't feel comfortable talking about it to anyone.

You must realize that taking things one day at a time will help you in the long run. It is about making small strides to get back where you once were. You will have setbacks and that is fine, the important thing is to not let those setbacks stop you from moving forward. Your days will be like the weather, clear and sunny one day then dark and stormy the next. It doesn't matter how bad things look, they will always get better. If you are having the worst day imaginable, relax, take some time to yourself, take a deep breath, listen to some music, or watch some television. They may or may not work but there is no harm in trying. Tell yourself that while this day is not going so well, there will be better ones to come. You will get stronger in the end and they will also help you appreciate the good days, when they come around, and they will.

Most of us that fight depression will have dark thoughts that others may not want to hear about. These are the days that we think about harming ourselves; I know because I have been there myself. The day is going bad and noting you can do or tell yourself seems to be helping your mood. It seems that there is no reason for you to keep fighting and you think it will be easier to just give up, not only on you, but on everyone else too. Sometimes you just want to disappear and not tell anyone where you are going; they don't love you and won't miss you anyway, right? Nothing could be further from the truth. They do love you and they will miss you. If they didn't care about you, they would have never offered to help you, check in on you, or take some time out their busy days to talk to you, even if it is a simple phone call, a text message, a chat session online, or if they send an eail.

I've often heard people who are depressed talk about committing suicide. You need to realize that while doing this might seem like a feasible option, you are leaving behind a path of sadness and destruction that might never end. Everyone will be asking why it came to this and if there was anything they'd missed. Families have been known to turn on each other or on the friends of the deceased. Children and young siblings will have to deal with it for the rest of their lives. They will never understand what happened and might even blame themselves. Spouses will also have a hard time coping with it and could possibly fall into a state of depression themselves, which could cause the whole thing to start all over again. Taking this course of action can impact many different people in many different ways. For your sake, and of those who love you, I really hope you don't give in to these dark thoughts. One day at a time might be a cliché, but it might also be the one thing you need to repeat to yourself when you are finding it difficult to keep moving forward.

REALIZE THAT IT IS A PART OF YOU

You have accepted that you need to take things one day at a time, so now what? You must realize that the depression is now a part of you and that you will need to constantly work at keeping it from creeping back in.

It doesn't matter how much time has lapsed since you went through it, the seed has been planted and will always be there. This doesn't mean that you can't live a happy and fulfilling life, it just means that since you have been through it once, you will be able to spot it in yourself and those around you if it decides to show its ugly face again. You can use it to your advantage and help others fight through it. You will be equipped to handle it better and you will be more understanding and sympathetic to those who are going through it for the first time. You might end up being the person they need in order to fight back. When I went through my bout of depression, I didn't have anyone who had been through it to talk to, but I can assure you that if I did, it would have made things easier to handle.

If public speaking is something you are capable of doing, forming a support group for others suffering or offering to counsel friends who wouldn't feel comfortable in large groups, are great ways to help. You know how bad things can get and being a voice for those who need it the most can also be very rewarding. There are many things you can do once you have been through it by simply understanding and accepting that it is a part of you. It doesn't have to be a bad thing because, as I pointed out, you can do so much good with it. Embrace it and don't be ashamed of it.

Use this to inspire others and give them hope so that if they ever go through it they know it can be beat. Volunteer to go to the local high schools where teens are facing peer pressure, stress from trying to fit in and other social issues and ask if you can tell your story in hopes of giving them some insight. Help them realize that depression is a common occurrence but with help it can be handled and overcome.

It has been over eight years since I have gone through my divorce and I still have some days where I don't want to be around anyone. I have some good days and I have some bad days. There are nights where I can't sleep and I have no idea why. I know that there is a possibility that it is a lingering effect of the depression I went through, but I won't allow it to come back full force. I still write my poetry when I feel there is something that needs to be said. When I am home alone I dive into my writing or will find something to watch. I can honestly say that, although I fought off the depression I felt all those years ago, I am still aware that it will be with me forever. I have friends who are going through it now and since I have felt what they are feeling I do my best to help them out. I will listen and offer some words of encouragement or try to make them laugh and forget their problems. I won't push them to talk to me, rather I let them decide when they are ready to open up and tell me what it is they are dealing with. I am happy with my life and I accept that depression is a part of me now, but I refuse to let it be a controlling part. I use the knowledge I gained from going through it to help those I can and to let them know that things will be ok.

I know this work won't be able to help everyone who is going through it, but if it can help just one person, then I will be happy with that. I sat down and wrote this to help those who need and want the help, as well as to offer some insight for those who don't know how to help a friend or loved one who is fighting depression. These are just my own personal thoughts and opinions.

I want you all to know that there is help out there available to everyone. Nobody needs to go through this alone, if you know someone who is suffering from depression please help them or find someone who can do it. If you are the one suffering from depression, don't be afraid to ask for help. Look around your local community or pick up the phone and call someone. Nowadays the information you need is available at your fingertips. Asking for help is not a sign of weakness; it is a sign of strength.

If you or someone you know is suffering from depression please seek help. Here are some places you can look into that I found online;

UNITED STATES NATIONAL SUICIDE PREVENTION LIFELINE

1 (800) 273-8255

Hours: 24 hours, 7 days a week
Languages: English, Spanish
Website: www.suicidepreventionlifeline.org

HEALTHLINE
http://www.healthline.com/health/depression/help-for-depression#TreatmentFacts1

ANXIETY AND DEPRESSION

ASSOCIATION OF AMERICA

http://www.adaa.org/finding-help

DEPRESSION CHAT ROOM

& HELP ONLINE

https://www.7cupsoftea.com/depression-help-online/

OTHER OPTIONS ARE AVAILABLE IN YOUR LOCAL AREA. SEEK OUT HELP WITH YOUR LOCAL CHURCHES OR COMMUNITY ORGANIZATIONS. TOGETHER WE CAN OVERCOME DEPRESSION.

Acknowledgements

"This Beautiful Escape" wouldn't have been possible without the help of some truly amazing people.

A big huge thank you to…

All the authors that contributed to the anthology and donated to the Ataxia Awareness Fundraiser. Your generosity will be what makes this fundraiser a success.

Taneil Currie for your fabulous inspirational story idea.

Darkmantle Designs for the Cover Art on "This Beautiful Escape Volume Two", formatting both books and your insight and expertise.

Chelle Bliss for the cover art on "This Beautiful Escape Volume One"

Muffy Wilson for recruiting some amazing authors, for promoting the fundraiser and all the memes you made.

David S. Scott, thank you for lighting a fire under me, for your research, the time you spent helping me get organized, dealing with the cover art and for being the voice of reason when I needed it.

Terrie Meerschaert for organizing the stories and quotes, for your tireless efforts and for your support.

Tammy Markowski for always being there if I needed help with anything and for the countless hours you spent contacting blogs.

Kaz Blonde for your generous donation to Ataxia Canada.

Anita Maynard for recruiting some awesome authors.

All the street teams, blogs and authors that helped get the word out.

Louise Evans for the beautiful teasers you made.

Airicka Phoenix, Amber Garcia and Aimee Shaye for all your help getting the word out.

Louisa Gray from Boom Books Promotions for hosting the fundraising event.

All the readers that will purchase this book to help support Ataxia Canada.

Komal Chandwani would like to make additional acknowledgments:

*Writing this story has been a journey of ups and downs, but in the end, it is all worth it. I hope that **Embrace** puts a smile on each reader's face and warms their heart with love.*

There are so many people I'd like to thank, but first and foremost, it is **Melissa Ann.** I am honoured to be a part of this anthology and without your support and positivity this wouldn't have been possible.

Thank you, **mom** for being there and supporting me through my writing journey. You believed in this story and here it is. Without your support I wouldn't have been able to accomplish what I had planned.

To my editors, **Anita Maynard and Vaibhavi Parmar**. You ladies have done a fantastic work on making this story come to life. Thank you for not laughing at my silly mistakes, but actually helping me out. I'm truly grateful.

Vaibhavi, thank you for not smacking me whenever I freaked out. You've helped me a lot on this story and I cannot thank you enough, love. All those last minute checking and editing have made this story what it is now.

My mentor, **JP Barry**. Your positivity and words of encouragement have helped me a lot. You help me improve every day. As I always say, you are good for my confidence. Thank you for looking out for me.

To my lovely friend, **Heather Dianne Weimer.** Thank you for reading this story. The constructive and honest feedback from your end is always appreciated. I know you are always happy to help and I love you for that.

To **Chelle Bliss**, thank you for designing such a beautiful cover and **Terrie Meerschaert and Darkmantle Designs** for the fabulous formatting.

Thank you everyone for supporting me and reading this story. ♥

Love, Komal xo

Heather Dahlgren would like to make additional acknowledgments:

I want to thank Melissa Ann for having a brilliant mind and bringing us all together. You are such an incredible woman and I'm honored to call you my friend.

Thank you to Sally's Sneaky Peek for proofreading for me. For being so amazing and getting it done so quickly. You are amazing.

I want to thank my family for helping me with my struggles and for letting me live of my dream of being an author.

To all the readers, thank you. Without you we are nothing. I hope you are able to take away inspiration from everything you read.

Made in the USA
Charleston, SC
20 December 2015